·Patrick Smith·

Riverhead Books
New York

ASK THE Pilot

. . .

Everything You
Need to Know
About Air Travel

. . .

RIVERHEAD BOOKS
Published by The Berkley Publishing Group
A division of Penguin Group (USA) Inc.
375 Hudson Street
New York, New York 10014

Copyright © 2004 by Patrick Smith
Book design by Tiffany Estreicher
Cover art and design by Ben Gibson

First Riverhead trade paperback edition: June 2004

Library of Congress Cataloging-in-Publication Data

Smith, Patrick, 1966–
   Ask the pilot : everything you need to know about air travel / Patrick Smith.—1st Riverhead trade paperback ed.
      p.   cm.
   ISBN 1-59448-004-4 (trade pbk.)
      1. Air travel.   2. Aeronautics, Commercial.   I. Title.

HE9776.S58   2004
910'.2'02—dc22

                                                          2004046675

Printed in the United States of America

CONTENTS

AIRFLEETS FOR NEOPHYTES

Airfoiled—the art of wings and keeping aloft · A primer on moving parts · Aerobatics in a 747? · Turbines and turbofans—an intro to jets and props · No engines? Can we glide to a landing? · Boeing versus Airbus · Too hot to handle, too high to fly? · Those white lines—clouds or conspiracy?

UP TO SPEED—THE PROMISE AND PERIL OF CONCORDE

Turbulence and windshear · Pressurization—how, why, and what if it's lost? · Are we running out of fuel? · How can ice crash a plane? · The truth about toilet water · Are we flying with broken parts? · Aging planes—how old is too old?

IDLEWILD, ROANOKE, AND TIMBUKTU TOO

Into the wind and backwards to boot · Takeoff trauma and the climbout cutback · V-what? · A runway nightmare—fact or fiction? · From whence the aborted takeoff? For what the aborted landing? · Foggy notions and crooked landings—finding the ground · Those mysteriously missing thunderstorms · SCROD, WOPPO, BOSOX, and Gardner · The biggest and busiest airports · To HEL and back

EN ROUTE ANGST AND THE PSYCHOLOGY OF FEAR

The ten worst crashes in history · Those dangerous foreign airlines? · Cockpits and culture · Fallacies and flotation—getting to know your life jacket · Crackpots and conspiracy · The true and false of shoulder-fired missiles · Crewless catastrophe—can a passenger land the plane? · Soft walls and other lousy ideas

MOURNING THE CHEAT LINE

The oldest, biggest, best, and worst carriers · What, no Africa? · Small countries, big airlines · Red-eye rationale · A code-share primer · The world's longest flight · Flight numbers, Shamrocks, Clippers, and Cacti

AUTHOR'S NOTE AND ACKNOWLEDGMENTS

The realm of commercial aviation is a landscape—or skyscape if you'd rather—of ever-shifting facts and statistics. Airlines come and go; planes are bought and sold; routes are swapped and dropped. Now and then comes a tragedy. I've done my best to ensure long-term timeliness of the information, but always bear in mind the nature of the business.

The Q & A sequences herein were provided by readers of my online column, to whom I am deeply grateful for their interest and encouragement. Certain questions are verbatim submissions; others I've adapted and revised for clarity.

. . .

I extend foremost gratitude to Sophia Seidner, whose clear thinking saved this project from ruin on more than one occasion. A similar debt is owed to the patience of Marc Haeringer and Amy Hertz at Riverhead Books.

Logistical and proofreading support was provided by the indispensable Julia Petipas. Creative liaison was Michael G. Kennedy. Research and consultation courtesy of Todd Gagerman, David

Walsh, Elizabeth and James Cradock, Douglas Hoeschle, Tom Daly, and John Mazor. Thanks also to Alex Beam and Deacon Blues. Acoustic accompaniments by Pat Fish and the Jazz Butcher Conspiracy.

Special acknowledgment to Andrew Leonard at Salon.com, without whose gamble on a cold call more than two years ago these pages would not exist.

The Painter's Brush

. . .

*"I must place on record my regret that the
human race ever learned to fly."*

—WINSTON CHURCHILL

We assume Churchill was thinking aerial bombardment and
Gatling guns, not overcrowded cabins, broken armrests, screaming
infants, or terrorism. I figure he had the Luftwaffe in mind; not a
tourist charter to Majorca. Six decades later, flight remains no less a
focus of curiosity, fear, and anxiety, if mainly, though not completely, for different reasons. Fair to say every passenger has a
question, a doubt, and probably a list of complaints in the back of
his or her mind.

The chapters that follow are a revised and adapted collection of
articles and columns written for an online magazine, Salon.com,
beginning in the winter of 2001 just after the World Trade Center
catastrophe. I was getting more and more irritated by distortions

and inaccuracies in the media's aviation reportage, and also by the less than captivating attempts of industry experts to set things straight. I grew bored with the dry swagger of the usual post-crash suspects—crew-cut FAA spokespeople, this or that retired TWA captain. They know their stuff, but always there was something missing—they were never speaking to, and never able to exploit, people's *general* sense of curiosity.

The purpose of this book is not to describe the metallurgy of a jet engine or the error tolerances of GPS navigation. It is not a book targeted for gearheads or aviation aficionados, and the intent is not to burden readers with jargon or tire them (or the author) with specs about airplanes. Neither is it a muckraking exposé or sensationalist tell-all. Herein you will find no lurid accounts of in-flight orgies or scary admonishments of danger.

Whether I consider myself more, or less, cerebral about flying than most pilots is open to debate. My enthrallment as a youngster was—and remains—with the workings of the airlines themselves. I have limited fascination with the sky; I feel no ecstatic glee at the breaking of any "surly bonds." In grade school I'd pore over the system maps and timetables of Pan Am, Aeroflot, Lufthansa, and British Airways, memorizing the names of the foreign capitals they flew to, then drawing up my own imaginary airlines and tracing out their intended routes. The sight of a Piper Cub meant nothing to me. Five minutes at an air show watching the Thunderbirds do barrel rolls and I was bored to tears. Airplanes helped me appreciate the world. They turned me on to geography, travel, and culture. By studying the airlines as a kid, I was inspired, later in life, to visit places like Botswana, Cambodia and India. It was a *direct* connection.

The disconnect between air travel and culture seems to me wholly unnatural, yet we've seen virtually a clean break. Nobody gives a damn anymore *how you get there*. I'll ask friends about trips they take, always wanting to know which airline and aircraft they rode on. Often enough the answer is "I don't remember." A shame for the means to be so coldly separated from the ends, for people to find travel so valuable and enriching, yet to deem irrelevant the tools that allow it to happen. For most, whether bound for Kansas or Kathmandu, the airplane is a necessary evil, *incidental* to the journey but no longer part of it.

Planes are complicated, sophisticated, and, dare the biased enthusiast submit, beautiful (some of them). This affinity isn't the adrenaline-charged passion some might feel at the sight of a muscle car, or the way a collector might coo lovingly while oiling the barrels of his handguns. Planes can be sexy, I say, but spare me the blather about phalluses and hormones. I'm talking about a passion that takes all of humanity into account: the world's airlines bridging the continents, linking nations and peoples of the world. If that sounds hokey or far-fetched, I propose a stroll through Kennedy airport during the nightly transatlantic departure push.

What's at the root of all this weepy culture bridging? The aircraft itself, the graceful ship docked outside that nobody is paying attention to. How many travelers with their passports full of stamps and visas can tell you the difference between an A340 and a

777? How many can tell you which is the world's oldest airline (KLM), the largest plane (still the 747), or whose face that is up on the tail of EgyptAir (it's Horus, the Egyptian sky god)?

An old girlfriend of mine, an artist who would have no trouble appreciating the play of light in a seventeenth-century painting by Vermeer, found all this utterly perplexing. While I could see urbane elegance in the lines of a jetliner, or a heady significance in the color scheme of a prestigious airline, she analogized airplanes not as works of art themselves, but merely as the tool. The sky was the canvas, the plane nothing less discardable than the painter's brush. I disagree, for as a brush's stroke represents the moment of artistic inspiration, what is travel without the *journey*?

As a kid during the mid 1970s, I remember when passengers still broke out in applause at every smooth landing. Travel by plane still clung to a sort of delusional esteem. If one could choose a single point at which the thrill was at last put to pasture, it would be the moment when, in the fall of 1978, President Carter put his name on the Airline Deregulation Act. In the years to come, deregulation unleashed a wave of upstart airlines. Most were doomed to failure, but they collectively sacked what was once coveted territory of the well-dressed and well-heeled—airports flung open like palaces of the czars.

The trouble is, not only did flying become cheaper and more accessible, but it became immensely more uncomfortable and tedious, prone to all the breakdown and hassle one might expect when 250 million people suddenly have free run at a particular infrastructure. The going cliché, as concourses grew more crowded, was a frustrated comparison of the airport terminal to the downtown bus station. How much longer before travelers have to endure the same dreary disrepair and stained seatbacks of the Greyhound depot? To properly relish the irony here, you need only pay a visit to Boston's renovated South Station, with its polished granite floors and skylights.

To be clear, I am not extolling the virtues of tiny seats or the culinary subtlety of half-ounce bags of snack mix. The idea is to show some beauty where you *don't expect it*. The indignities of flying aside, there are, at least for now, still many jewels, both aesthetic and existential, to be found. To counter them with yet more horror stories from row 37 would be as boring as my laying out the schematics of a plane's electrical system. Okay, flying sucks, but if you can't value the *idea* of zipping to Hong Kong in twelve hours in a million-pound machine, there's a problem.

Rarely do you come across an American who has never flown in an airplane, and we've come to treat flying with ho-hum embrace as yet another impressive but ultimately uninspiring technological realm. This is the ultimate realization, perhaps, of a fully evolved technology, whereby flying itself has become secondary to the experience in whole. Here I am, sitting in a Boeing 747, a plane that if tipped onto its nose, would rise as tall as a twenty-story office tower. I'm at 33,000 feet over the Pacific Ocean, traveling at six hundred miles-per-hour bound for the Far East, a voyage that once took seven weeks in a sailing ship. And what are the passengers doing? Complaining, sulking, reading the paper, and tapping grumbly rants into their laptops. The man next to me, having paid a $6,900 business class fare, is upset over a dent in his can of ginger ale.

Progress, one way or the other, mandates the extraordinary become the ordinary. In the case of commercial aviation, luxury and privilege were distilled into vinegar for the masses. But don't we lose valuable perspective on our own capabilities and triumphs when we begin to equate the commonplace, more or less by definition, with the tedious? Don't we forfeit a bit of our pride when we sneer indifferently at the sight of a jet airplane—something that is, at heart, a world-changing triumph of industrial design?

My aim is to make you think so, though you may be tempted, as one person was, to call me a "bonehead" and demand the bankruptcy of each and every airline for wedging you into such a tiny space and expecting you to eat such crappy food. Another writes mockingly, "Sure, I should feel so goddamn lucky to fly," taking me to task for daring to ask the public to, gulp, *appreciate* the chance to voyage across oceans and continents with all the circumstance of motoring to the mall. Actually, yes, you should feel lucky.

Once upon a time, of course, you'd have had a five-course meal served by a tuxedoed steward, and a smoking lounge where you could sit in a big reclining chair, maybe chatting with Farouk before retiring to your private sleeping berth. But in 1939 aboard Pan Am's *Dixie Clipper*, it cost $375 to fly each way between New York and France. This is lost on the great unwashed, who today, wearing flip-flops, can traverse the Atlantic in a quarter-billion dollar jetliner for $259. And if you're insatiably eager to revisit those indulgences of years past, you can do that too, by purchasing a first- or business-class ticket at a fraction of the cost of fifty years ago.

And you'll get there four times as fast.

Things About Wings and Why Knots?

· · ·

AIRFLEETS FOR NEOPHYTES

In the second grade my two favorite toys were Boeing 747s. The first was an inflatable replica—similar to one of those novelty balloons you buy at parades—with rubbery wings that drooped in such violation of the real thing that I taped them into position. At nine years old the oversized toy seemed enormous, like my own personal Macy's float.

Second was a small plastic airplane about a foot long with rubber wheels. Like the balloon, it was decked out in the livery of Pan Am, and even carried the name and registration of the airline's flagship jumbo, *Clipper America*. One side of the fuselage was transparent, made of clear polystyrene through which an entire interior, row-by-row and seat-by-seat, could be viewed. The blue and red pastels of the tiny chairs is something I can still picture exactly.

What most infatuated me was the spiral staircase, modeled in perfect plastic miniature near the toy plane's nose. Early-version 747s were always outfitted with a set of spiral stairs, leading from the forward boarding door to the plane's famous upper deck, a design quirk that became an iconic representation of the airplane. When in 1982 I took my first trip on a real 747, I beamed at the sight of the winding column of steps, materializing just beyond the El Al purser who greeted me at the end of the Jetway. It gave the entranceway the look and feel of a lobby, like the grand vestibule of an ocean liner.

To this day, the association is one I can't escape. When I notice the twisting iron fire escape of an old factory, I think 747. In the At Home section of the Sunday paper, with a spread of some chic downtown loft, there it is again. Those stairs are in my blood—a genetic helix spinning upward to a kind of pilot Nirvana. (Alas, updated 747s adopted a traditional, ladder-style staircase.)

In the mid-1990s, Boeing ran an advertisement in *Air Transport World* for its most famous product, the 747. The ad was a two-pager, with a nose-on silhouette of the plane against a dusky orange sunset. "*Where/does this/take you?*" asked Boeing across the centerfold. Below this: "*A stone monastery in the shadow of a Himalayan peak. A cluster of tents on the sweep of the Serengeti plains. The Boeing 747 was made for places like these. Distant places filled with adventure, romance, and discovery.*" I so related to this syrupy bit of corporate PR that I clipped it from the magazine and kept it in a cardboard folder. Whenever it seemed my career was going nowhere, which was all the time, I'd pull out the ad and look at it.

In league with the Concorde, the 747 is one of the only true Jet Age celebrities. Not bad for a design conceptualized in the 1960s as a military cargo plane. In '67 the government went instead with

Lockheed and its C-5 Galaxy. Somehow "Galaxy" is so over-the-top. There's something more dignified in Boeing's numberings—the tilt of the 7s, the simple palindromic ring: Seven-forty-seven.

It was a friend of mine, not me, who became the first pilot I knew to fly one, setting off for Shanghai and Taipei while I flew to Hartford and Harrisburg. Closest I got was the occasional upstairs seating assignment. The upper deck is a cozy, private room with an arched ceiling like the inside of a miniature hangar. I'd recline up there, basking in the self-satisfaction of having made it, at least in one way, up the spiral stairs. I had an upper-deck seat en route to Nairobi in 1987 on British Airways. Prior to pushback I wandered into the cockpit unannounced, to have a look and thinking the guys might be interested to learn they had a newly licensed pilot on-board. They weren't. I'd interrupted the three-way choreography of their before-start checklist, and they asked me to go away and slammed the door. "Yes, we *do* mind," snapped the second officer in a voice exactly like Graham Chapman.

Right now, Northwest and United are the only 747 operators in the USA (not including a couple of freight companies), but over-seas they remain common. As of 2003 Boeing had built more 747s than either 767s or 757s, with multiple modifications to the '69 original, and well into the 1990s it accounted for a third of Boeing's profits. For now it remains the largest, and to me the world's pret-tiest, airliner, though I'm sure you've heard word of the Airbus double-decker, the A380, slated for launch with Singapore Airlines in 2006. As Boeing did three decades ago, Airbus is staking its fu-ture on a new megaplane.

At more than a million pounds takeoff weight, the A380 shall knock the 747 to second place after a thirty-seven-year reign. Impressive, and you can bet the premiere will be accompanied by headlines, footage, and maybe its own hour or two on the Discovery Channel. But while not to squelch the excitement, it won't be revolutionary. When the 747 rolled from the hangar in 1969, it was more than *twice* the size of the largest existing airplane, and was alone a whole new concept—the widebody jet. For better or worse, this was the machine whose economies of scale ushered in the age of affordable long-haul travel. The A380 is only a third or so bigger than a 747, and for the most part will rely on existing infrastructures. And size isn't everything; what truly chagrins me is the way this plane will look—a bulbous, ungainly craft without any of the 747's elegance.

Hot on its heels is Boeing's 7E7 "Dreamliner," an advanced, ultra-efficient, 200-plus seater scheduled for entry around 2008. It'll be Boeing's first all-new design since the 777, and by most accounts a do or die move for a plane maker whose catalog has grown stagnant. Boeing says the 7E7 will be "eco-friendly and people friendly." So people-friendly, in fact, that its future passengers got to name it. The name they chose, via an online poll, was to me a matter of some revulsion, though I guess Dreamliner was better than other proposed options (Stratoclimber, eLiner). Then again, maybe an ugly plane deserves an ugly name. Dreamliner looks to be a mix between a 767 and an amusement park ride, with a forehead like a porpoise.

While the humpbacked 747 is readily distinguishable even to casual flyers, most airplanes are not. Distinctive, if obnoxious, exceptions like the A380 or Dreamliner aside, most designs have become insipidly generic. With but two remaining producers, Boeing and Airbus, it seems the shrunken gene pool has stuck us with a lineage of inbred lookalikes. In grade school I was adept at pointing out the differences between a DC-9 and a 727 from six miles out, a skill that both amazed (occasionally) and annoyed (always) the other kids. This is a lost art thanks to the similarities of later-generation jets.

I beg to differ that, as one designer put it, "air does not yield to style." Must modern planes, by aerodynamic necessity, lack even vaguely assertive aesthetics? I once watched an Airbus A320 taxi past an airport window, and as it did so three women sitting alongside me burst out in a collective giggle. "What a goofy little plane." And you've got to admit, the A320 is something less than elegant, a kind of utilitarian caricature that looks like it might have popped from an Airbus vending machine, or maybe hatched from an egg laid by a 747.

I point out exceptions, such as the A320's big brother, the urbane A340. Unlike most of its counterparts from the past twenty-five years, the A340 has four engines instead of the standard two, but just because a plane has two engines does it *need* to be ugly? Why can't an attractive and distinctive profile, like that of the long-forgotten Caravelle, be revived with a modern twist?

Call it pop aviation culture. I believe corporate unwillingness and lack of imagination, not the rules of aerodynamics, are responsible for so many uninspired copycats. That's romantically cynical of me, of course, as the standardization and interchangeability of parts and assembly lines make for better use of resources and steadier profits.

Current jetliners are the product of two main camps, Seattle-grown Boeing and Europe's Airbus Industrie consortium. It wasn't always this way. For years we had McDonnell Douglas and various throw-ins from North America and abroad: Lockheed, Convair, British Aerospace, Fokker. And we shan't neglect the Russians. Things are quiet now, but the design bureaus at Antonov, Ilyushin, and Tupolev assembled thousands of jets over the decades. While the bulk of these were Western knockoffs turned Cold War pumpkins, many are still in service, namely in the former Russian republics. A couple of newer prototypes were recently introduced, destined for sale to ex-Aeroflot directorates.

Regional aircraft have come from a slew of builders and countries. Canada's Canadair (now belonging to the Bombardier entity) and Brazil's Embraer make the two most popular regional jets—RJs in the language—while turboprops have been exported from Sweden, Holland, Spain, France, and Indonesia. Even the Czechs manufactured a popular seventeen-seater.

America's first jet was the Boeing 707, third in commercial service behind England's star-crossed Comet and the Soviet's TU-104. The 707 debuted between Idlewild and Orly (that's New York and Paris) with Pan Am in 1959. Boeing has since delivered the 727 through 777. The numbers have nothing to do with size and pertain only to order of construction. There also was a kind of short-bodied 707 called a 720. They skipped the 717 (see below), though the designation was initially reserved for a military version of the 707.

From Airbus have come the A300 through A340, with the A380 in fine-tuning as we speak. Nobody knows what happened to the A350 through A370. Plenty of people, I've learned, think of an Airbus as a single plane, when in fact, like those from Boeing, it's a series ranging from skinny hundred-seaters to long-ranging wide-bodies. The consortium's only head-turner, if you ask me, is the A340. Like the Concorde, it possesses a certain anthropomorphic quality, with its aristocratic posture and coyly upturned winglets. Hundreds have been sold, but Air Canada remains the only North American operator.

Minor variations of the Airbus types are enough to make even a veteran plane spotter berserk. The A300-600 is really just an extended A310. An A319 is nothing more (or less) than a smaller A320, further reduced into the A318. Then there's the A321. The new-style mishmash of numbers, in this traditionalist's opinion, cheapens everything. That each model wasn't simply given a "dash" suffix is irritating. On our side of the ocean, at least a 737-800 is still a 737. But then, when Boeing ate up McDonnell Douglas, it took the MD95, which was really just a souped-up MD90, which was really just a souped-up DC-9, and *re*-christened it, lo and behold, the Boeing 717. So much for numerical chronology. The DC-9, first flown in 1965, is now brand-new, as it were, as the 717.

Some planes have carried stand-alone designations, like the Comet; others had nicknames in conjunction with numbers, like Lockheed's L-1011 TriStar. There's the BAC/British Aerospace One-Eleven, which in its proper spelled-out form is both a name *and* a number. Most were good choices, understated and poetic: Constellation, Trident, Vanguard, Concorde. The English laid it on thick with the Britannia, a turboprop of the 1950s, but mainly we've been treated to dignity and restraint. Dreamliner will change that.

With numbers, the progressive series always worked best—the 707 through 777, the DC-1 through DC-10. Eventually things got weird. Airbus jumped four places with no explanation, and McDonnell Douglas abandoned DC for MD, scrambling up the numbers for good measure. Everyone's heard of a DC-9, but what the hell is an MD-80? Answer: it's a modernized DC-9. Everyone knows of the DC-10, but what the hell is an MD-11? Answer: it's a modernized DC-10. And so on.

At least we haven't got planes called "Camry" or "Passat."

So how do heavy metal tubes with tons of passengers and cargo stay in the air?

Yes, the semiwhimsical musing that forms the philosophical kernel of every layperson's curiosity about airplanes. But the answer is an easy one: Next time you're driving down the highway in your Honda, stick your hand out the window, parallel to the ground, and fly it along like a wing. Bend it upward slightly, and it rises, no?

I'll be chided for a less-than-nuanced explanation, but truly that's the gist of it. Orville Wright said it like this: "The airplane stays up because it doesn't have the time to fall." Not getting the Accord off the ground? Okay, but now imagine your hand is really, really big, and the car has enough horsepower to go really, really fast. Becoming airborne is all about procuring the right surpluses among the four competing forces of flight—enough thrust over drag, and enough lift over weight. The size of the airplane—no matter how awe-inspiring, or even disconcerting, is irrelevant.

There's also something in Flying 101 known as Bernoulli's Principle, named for Daniel Bernoulli, an eighteenth-century Swiss mathematician who never saw an airplane. When forced through a constriction or across a curved surface, a fluid will accelerate and its pressure will simultaneously decrease. Our fluid is air, which moves faster over the top of the wing, which is curved (less pressure), than it does along the flatter surface below (higher pressure). The resulting upward push contributes to lift.

Loss of lift is a stall. Different areas of a wing will stall at different values, but the basic idea is easily demonstrated back on the highway: Tilt your hand a little too steeply, or brake the Honda below a certain point, and your arm ceases to fly.

But one look at the details of a wing tells me it's more complicated than that.

Planes achieve optimum economy during cruise flight. That's at high altitudes and just shy of the sound barrier for some jets. Honing this efficiency is an art—grist for the engineers and their wind tunnels. The lateral cross section of a wing, around which the air does its thing, is called an airfoil, and it's meticulously sculpted. That straight, blockish wing of your average thirty-seater is a lot more high-tech than you think. Not only in cross section, but spanwise too—the curvature and thickness changing from root to tip.

Wings are augmented with an array of supplemental components—namely flaps and slats, and spoilers—for life at low speeds. Powered by hydraulics, they are most elaborate on faster aircraft, but all commercial planes have some version of them. I remember one of my first plane trips, on a 727, in a window seat just behind the wing, how the entire structure seemed to disassemble itself during descent. Big, triple-slotted flaps came barreling down, the spoilers and ailerons fluttering and waving, while up front the slats and leading edge flaps dropped into position. Magically, almost, you could see right *through* the very center of the wing, like through the bones of a skeletonized animal, with houses and trees appearing where the sections had slid apart.

Flaps trail backward and downward, enhancing the wing's camber for safe, stable flight at lesser velocities. Airliners take off and land with flaps extended, though exact settings will vary. There are inboard and outboard subsets, which themselves can be segmented horizontally. Slats roll forward from a wing's forward edge and perform a similar function. There can be several, deployed separately or together as needed.

Spoilers are rectangular planks that spring from the wing's upper surface. There can be a half dozen or so on each side, and their use is most clearly seen on touchdown, when they pop to full deflection to assist in deceleration. A raised spoiler greatly disturbs airflow across the wing, reducing lift while simultaneously adding copious amounts of drag. In flight, spoilers are used to increase rates of descent and decrease airspeed.

Remembering Bernoulli, when a wing cuts through the sky, molecules of air accelerate across its camber. As this acceleration reaches the speed of sound, a shock wave builds along the surface, killing lift. Sweeping the wings backward induces a more agreeable, spanwise flow. On faster planes you'll find a sweep greater than 40 degrees; the slowest have almost no sweep at all. Swept wings have terrible low-speed characteristics, requiring complex flaps and slats.

Canting wings upward from the root counteracts an inherent, side-to-side rolling and yawing tendency. This tilt, most easily seen from a nose-on perspective, is called dihedral. The Soviets, ever the good contrarians, used to apply an opposite but equally effective version called anhedral, canting their wings downward.

And no, by the way, an airliner cannot fly with one wing. An Israeli fighter jet once survived having a wing torn away, but your 757 will not. Components—everything from navigational systems to engines—often exist in duplicate or triplicate, but this spirit of redundancy cannot extend to something so wholly integral to flight itself. So, it's all in the wing. A plane is built around its wings the way a car is built around a chassis or a bicycle around a frame. Great big wings produce great big amounts of lift, enough to get a 747, at nearly a million pounds, off the ground once it hits about 150 knots.

What's a knot?

In his story *A Supposedly Fun Thing I'll Never Do Again*, David Foster Wallace is on a cruise ship where he's repeatedly perplexed by mention of "knots," unable to figure out exactly what they are. Simple enough: A knot, used both at sea and in the air, is a mile per hour. Except it's a nautical mile, not a statute one. Nautical miles are slightly longer (6,082 feet versus 5,280). Thus a hundred knots is slightly faster than a hundred miles per hour.

A nautical mile represents one-sixtieth of a degree of longitude along the equator. With sixty miles to each degree, we compute 360 degrees and 21,600 nautical miles of equatorial earthly circumference. The homonymic between knot and nautical is, well, *not* the right idea. The words sound alike, but haven't always meant the same thing. The original definition of knot goes back to when lengths of knotted rope were tossed from a ship to figure distances. Eventually, these more literal knots were equated to nautical miles.

Flaps and slats aside, I'm baffled by the moving parts of a plane's exterior. I see panels that move up and down, ones on the tail that go side to side, and others.

When a bird needs to maneuver, it does so by twisting its wings and tail, something pioneer aviators emulated by incorporating wing-bending in early aircraft. But airplanes today are made from aluminum and high-strength composites, not wood, fabric, or feathers. Operated hydraulically, electrically, and/or manually via cables, various moveable contrivances are fitted that let us climb, descend, and turn.

Atop the rear fuselage is the tail, or vertical stabilizer, which functions exactly as its presence suggests—to keep the plane straight. Hinged to the tail's back edge is the rudder. Unlike a boat, the rudder complements but does not control turns; the function is chiefly one of stability, tempering side-to-side swerve or yaw. Pilots move the rudder by means of foot pedals. That sounds quaint, and in reality the autopilot and an apparatus known as a yaw damper do most of the labor. Flying a four-seater requires some literal legwork, but pretty infrequently do you wrassle with the pedals of an airliner. Some rudders are divided into different sections, each with built-in limits pertaining to airspeed and angles of travel.

Beneath the tail, or occasionally attached to it, are two small wings. These are the horizontal stabilizers, the moveable rear portions of which are called elevators. The elevators command a plane's nose-up and nose-down pitch. Climbs and descents are also controlled by thrust, but for practical purposes elevators are what point the nose up or down, as directed by the forward or aft motion of the cockpit wheel or joystick.

Ailerons, located at the trailing edges of the wings, are responsible for turns. Pilots steer via the wheel or stick, which directs the ailerons up or down. They are interconnected and apply opposing forces: When the aileron on the left goes up, the one on the right goes down. A raised aileron reduces lift on that side, dropping the respective wing, while a lowered one causes the reverse. The smallest twitch of an aileron provides a good deal of turn, so you won't always spot them moving. It might look as though a plane is banked without anything having budged, but the ailerons have done their thing, if ever so slightly. Most large planes have two ailerons per wing, inboard and outboard, working in pairs or independently as airspeed dictates. They are often linked to the spoilers, which partially deploy to aid turning.

As you can see, a simple turn is a choreography of rudder, aileron, and spoiler. But before you picture a hapless pilot kicking his feet and grasping madly for levers, keep in mind many individual pieces are linked to single controls, so that a turn of the wheel or lowering of a lever will cause any combo of movements outside. And for much of a flight, it's the autopilot coordinating the physics. During approach and landing you'll often see spoilers lifting and retracting in rapid succession. This isn't the captain jamming things up and down, but the flight control systems making small, automatic adjustments.

Adding to the confusion, rudders, elevators and ailerons are equipped with smaller tabs that operate independently from the main surfaces. These "trim" tabs fine tune the motions of pitch, roll, and yaw.

If you're still with me, and before committing this all to memory, you'll be thrilled to know there are idiosyncratic variants of almost everything just described. One plane I flew had spoilers used only after landing, others that assisted with turning, and others still for inflight deceleration. And certain Boeing models are equipped not only with conventional trailing edge flaps, but ones at the leading edge too, in addition to slats. The Concorde had no horizontal stabilizers, so it had no elevators. But it did have "elevons." We'll save these, along with "flaperons," for another time.

A friend of mine, obviously intoxicated, claims he sat next to a dead-heading (off-duty) pilot who told him an airplane can be going too fast and too slow at the same time.

A plane stalls when, roughly put, the wing runs out of lift. Not only are there low-speed stalls, but high-speed "shock stalls" as well. As seen in the last question, when airflow over the wing nears the speed of sound, a shock wave builds atop the wing, disrupting the airflow and destroying lift. A stall. It's not only a question of how fast the plane itself is moving, but how fast the *air is moving around the wing*. Thus, at upper altitudes, where the air is very thin, a plane can find itself caught in an aerodynamic paradox: the higher it flies, the faster it needs to go to maintain lift; but the faster it goes, the closer it gets to that shock wave. You're stuck between going too fast and too slow at (almost) the same time. But relax. This is more of a theoretical illustration than anything passengers need to think about during that eerie calm over the ocean. It only happens at the limits of the performance envelope, which is not where airliners hang around. Crews calculate buffer speeds to keep them at a safe distance from this proverbial razor's edge

I notice many newer airplanes have those little upturned fins at the ends of their wings. What are the advantages of this design?

At a wing's tip, the higher pressure beneath meets the lower pressure above, sending out a turbulent discharge of air. Winglets, as they're affectionately called, help smooth this mixing, decreasing drag and, in turn, improving range and efficiency. You see them in different forms—some are rakishly canted while others, like those on the 767-400, are just a gentle tweak.

Because planes have different aerodynamic fingerprints, winglets aren't always cost-effective. Looking at some of the latest designs, the 747-400 and A340 have them, while the 777 does not. Other times they're sold as an option. An airline considers if the long-term fuel savings is worth the cost of installation. It depends on the flying. In Japan, Boeing has sold a number of 747-400s, used specifically on short-range pairings, with winglets *removed*. Aesthetics are a personal issue. I find winglets very attractive on some planes, like the A340, and ridiculous on others, like the 737-800.

Can a 747 fly a loop?

Any airplane can perform more or less any maneuver, theoretically, from loops to barrel rolls to a reverse inverted hammerhead Immelman. Whether it's a good idea is another story. Airliner components are not designed for aerobatics and may suffer damage—or worse—if forced into such scenarios. Plus, the cleaners would be up all night scrubbing out coffee stains and vomit. During a demonstration flight in the late 1950s, a Boeing 707 was intentionally flown upside down.

You've written that your duty isn't to burden readers with jargon. "A discussion of how a jet engine works," you've said, "is guaranteed to be uninteresting." If you don't mind, how *does* a jet engine work?

Picture the engine's anatomy as a back-to-back assembly of geared, rotating discs—compressors and turbines. Air is pulled in and directed through the spinning compressors. It's squeezed tightly, mixed with vaporized kerosene, and ignited. The combusted gases then come roaring out the back. Before they're expelled, a series of rotating turbines absorbs some of the energy. The turbines power the compressors and the large fan at the front of the nacelle. Older engines derived almost all of their thrust directly from the hot exploding gases. On modern ones that big forward fan does most of the work, and you can think of a jet as a kind of ducted fan, spun by a core of turbines and compressors.

The most powerful motors made by Rolls-Royce, General Electric, and Pratt & Whitney generate in excess of 100,000 pounds of thrust. The thrust is tapped to supply the electrical, hydraulic, pressurization, and deicing systems. Hence the term *powerplant*.

What is a turboprop?

All modern, propeller-driven commercial airliners are turboprops. A turboprop engine is, at heart, a jet. In this case, for better efficiency at lower altitudes and along shorter distances, the compressors and turbines drive a propeller rather than generate thrust directly. Loosely put, it's a jet-powered propeller. Hence the name jet-prop, sometimes used in lieu. There are no pistons in a turboprop engine, and the prefix shouldn't elicit confusion with turbocharging in the style of an automobile. Turboprops are safer and more reliable than pistons, and offer a more advantageous power-to-weight ratio. They're also expensive, which is why most private planes don't have them.

Jets and turboprops run on jet fuel, which is kerosene, a permutation of the stuff that powers camping lanterns. It's manufactured in different grades, but the flavor used by the airlines is called Jet-A. Televised fireballs notwithstanding, jet fuel is surprisingly stable and less combustible than you'd think, at least until atomization. You can stick a lit match into a puddle and it will not ignite. (Neither Patrick Smith nor the publisher shall be responsible for injuries or damage caused in connection to this statement.) In case you're dying to know, a gallon of Jet-A weighs about 6.7 pounds, varying with temperature.

I notice a hole up under the tail that emits some kind of exhaust. What is this?

That's the APU (auxiliary power unit), a small engine used to supply electricity, cooling, etc., when the main engines aren't running, or to supplement them when they are. All modern airliners, some turboprops included, have one, and it's typically located in the rear fuselage under the tail. If you're boarding through the old-style airstairs and notice a hissing, jetlike noise similar to the sound of ten thousand hairdryers, that's the APU.

It also provides compressed air for starting the main engines. Crews turn on the APU via the ship's batteries, and air is then piped to the compressors to get them turning. The first airliner with an APU as stock equipment was the 727, which debuted in 1964. Until then, high-pressure air was plumbed in via external supply. The old DC-8 I flew needed one of these so-called "air carts" at every departure. Some small jets and turboprops are started electrically. With no APU, an external GPU (ground power unit) gives the juice. Towed behind a small tractor, the GPU looks like one of those generators used at roadside construction sites. Unless in a pinch, a plane's internal batteries aren't used because the power draw is so strong.

If the APU is supplying ground power, why, then, do you often see the engines turning while a plane rests at the gate? Isn't that a waste of fuel?

Planes almost never run their engines at the gate. What you see is the wind spinning the first-stage turbofan. Even a moderate breeze can rotate that fan quite rapidly. If this seems impossible because a plane is cornered against a building or facing the wrong direction, that's because the wind is coming *from behind*. On newer engines, the majority of intake air is blown *around* the core of compressors and turbines, providing a clear shot at the fan blades from the rear. Wind blows through this duct, between core and cowl, and sets the assembly in motion.

If a large commercial jet loses total engine power, can it glide to a landing, or is it all over?

Complete engine loss, about as probable as a flight attendant volunteering to give you a shoe shine, is a full-blown dire emergency. Yet there's no more a prospect of instant calamity than taking your foot off the accelerator when coasting downhill in a car. The car keeps going and a plane will too. In fact, the power-off performance of a large jet is better than that of a light Piper or Cessna. It needs to glide at a considerably higher speed, but the ratio of distance covered to altitude lost—close to a 20:1 ratio—is almost double.

While it may surprise you, it's not the least bit uncommon for jets to descend at what a pilot would call idle thrust, i.e. with the engines run back to a zero-power condition. They're still operating, but providing very little push—not a lot different from switching them off entirely. You've been gliding without knowing it. There were a couple of infamous cases, one involving a 767, the other an A330, where planes lost all power and glided to a fatality-free touchdown.

I'm impressed by the sheer complexity of an airliner's cockpit. How can you possibly maintain watch over such an array of technology?

What looks at first like a Byzantine array is actually several distinct subsets, and many cockpit implements are rarely touched (unless it's in the simulator, where the sweaty smudge of many a nervous pilot's finger is found on those red-guarded switches not routinely needed). Much of what you see controls the anatomy of what pilots refer to collectively as "the systems." That's shoptalk for electrical, hydraulic, pressurization, and fuel, just to name a few. Then we've got navigational computers, and controls and displays for the engines. Not to mention the instruments pertaining to flight itself—altimeters, airspeed indicators, and so forth, often in duplicate or triplicate. On aircraft designed within the past twenty years, most of the old knobs, gauges, and dials are incorporated into software and presented on multiuse cockpit screens, either the CRT (cathode ray tube) variety, or, in more state-of-the-art cases, LCD (liquid crystal display).

Taxiing, taking off, climbing, descending, landing, and parking all come with tasks to be verified, and to this end different checklists are read aloud. Well before leaving the gate a crew will have run through several dozen callouts and confirmations. The checklists themselves exist as hardcopy cards or they're presented on the cockpit control screens. Yes, pilots really do say "check," like in the movies (and "roger" too), mixed with a litany of "armed," "on," "set," and many others.

In the days when three-pilot crews were the norm, the execution of a checklist was a kind of poetry, the three players responding to cues in an arcane, triangular ballet. The back-and-forth of a two-pilot cockpit is a less interesting performance.

So how much does an airliner cost, exactly?

Would you believe over $165 million for a single new Airbus A340 or Boeing 777? Or $50 million for a new 737? Even the little regional planes—a.k.a. commuters—that most of you can't stand also are multi-million-dollar machines, and you can remember that the next time you're walking up the stairs and cracking a joke about rubber bands. Twenty million dollars isn't out of the question for a high-end regional jet. Here are some starting list prices for new ships from Boeing, which should put the kibosh on your airline start-up dreams:

737-800: $58 million
757-200: $153 million
767-300: $116 million
747-400: $185 million

But an old 727 rebuilt as a freighter might run $2 million or less. It differs markedly with age, upgrades, and so on. A lot depends on the engines, which sell for millions apiece, and maintenance—how long before an overhaul is due, and what kind of overhaul? A used Airbus A320 might be had for $30 million. A five-year-old 767 is market valued at about $50 million, a 1993-vintage 757 around $17 million.

Airlines often do not own their planes outright. They lease them from banks and leasing companies, making regular payments not unlike the way you'd finance a car. There would be no other way to afford them. From an investor's view, the overall worth of an airline (say a billion dollars for a major), is far less than the combined book value of its equipment.

Do you think there is a difference in the quality of Boeing aircraft versus Airbus? I get the impression Airbus planes are made more cheaply, and they sound that way too—loud and tincanny. Boeings seem much more solid, quieter, and don't rattle as much.

I despise this question, and it comes up all the time in slippery forms. Descriptions like "tincanny" belittle the complexity of an airliner, no matter the maker. When I accuse the ATR of being "fragile," or if I call my old DC-8 a "relic," this is a pilot being colloquial. The ATR is not a Yugo, and neither, even by the most lenient extrapolation, is an Airbus.

Exposure to noise, and the *kind* of noise, depends greatly on where you're sitting and the position of the engines. On planes with wing-mounted turbofans, those seated closer to the front will hear a very distinctive grinding sound that emanates from the engine's fans and compressors, while a louder, whooshing roar is heard in the back. In planes like the MD-80, with aft-mounted engines, takeoff noise is almost nonexistent in the forward rows.

Airbuses and Boeings are different in many ways. It's not unlike comparing Apple to IBM, and each has its diehards who hate crossing over. Different planes abide by different philosophies of construction and operation, with all manner of pleasant and annoying quirks within. It gets technical. Opinions on which is the "better" plane get into the nuts and bolts of the systems—the kinds of details that'll have you (and me) yawning fast, and that do *not* reveal themselves as bangs, moans, or rattles. It comes down to preferences and, in a way, style, more than quality or lack thereof. There is no statistical safety difference that merits citing. In the end it's probably a wash. It ought to be when it's $60 million for your choice of a 737 or A320. At those costs, nobody could get away with selling junk.

I have to travel from Louisville to New York, but the only planes serving this route are puddle jumper regional jets. I'm reluctant to fly on these because I've heard they are unsafe. Are they?

I can't cure claustrophobia or speak to absence of legroom, but the size of an airliner has little or no bearing on how likely it is to crash. The metric correlating size with safety is a tough one to uproot (similar to the erroneous assumption that SUVs are safer than small cars). Here it delves into statistical minutiae, and thus "unsafe" becomes, for all intents and purposes, a useless expression. Regional jets—which seat anywhere from thirty to seventy or so people— are at least as sophisticated as many larger planes. An RJ like those from Bombardier or Embraer can have a sticker price in excess of $20 million. Pilots bristle at the term "puddle jumper" the way an environmental scientist would bristle at "tree hugger." Offhand— and I follow these things closely—I can think of only two RJ accidents in the past ten years. Thousands operate daily free of mishap.

How much do planes weigh?

A Boeing 747's maximum takeoff weight can be as high as 875,000 pounds, and the Airbus A380 will break the million mark. A fully packed 757 might be 250,000 pounds, while a fifty-passenger turboprop or regional jet will top out around 60,000. There are limits for the different operational regimes, including ones for sitting at the gate, taxiing, taking off, and landing. (The constraining factor for takeoff or landing is not necessarily the structural restriction of the plane, but more on that later.)

You might be amazed to learn that in the case of a 747, three hundred passengers and their suitcases—about 65,000 pounds en masse—make up less than *10 percent* of the total maximum bulk. Most of the weight comes from fuel. Because fuel is such a large percentage of overall weight, pilots rarely think of their kerosene in terms of gallons, but almost always as pounds. Everything from initial fueling to en-route burn is added or subtracted by weight, not volume. A fuel load of, say, 200,000 pounds (about 30,000 gallons) may be a third or more of a widebody airplane's sum heft.

Pilots are trained in the particulars of weight and balance, but in practice the grunt work is taken care of electronically, presented to the crew in dot matrix splendor with the rest of the preflight docket. Both weight and its distribution are important. A flight's center of gravity, which shifts as fuel is consumed, is calculated and kept track of.

If weight so affects performance, how is it ascertained with any degree of accuracy?

Passengers are not required to divulge the quantitative specs of their waistlines, obviously, and instead airlines use standard approximations for people and luggage. The values—presently 190 pounds per person (including carry-ons) and thirty per checked bag—are adjusted slightly higher during winter to account for heavier clothing (please don't ask me about transclimate routes). The boarding tallies are added to something called the BOW—Basic Operating Weight—which is a book value of the ship itself, replete with all furnishings, supplies, and crew. Compounded with fuel and cargo, the result is the total gross "ramp" weight. Fuel anticipated for taxiing is subtracted to reveal the takeoff weight.

After the crash of a nineteen-seater in Charlotte, North Carolina, in 2003, ten pounds were added to the passenger standard and five to the luggage. What happened in Charlotte was not, as news reports led the public to think, a consequence of an overweight or out-of-balance condition, but it nonetheless drew attention to the topic. The government responded by acknowledging our expanding waistlines.

Flying from Phoenix, the temperature topped 105 degrees and several passengers were bumped. We were told it was too hot for the plane to fly fully loaded. Can this be true? Is a plane so delicate that a few degrees render it unflyable?

This is one of those cases where airlines could do themselves great favor with coherent, explicit explanations instead of a churlish, "It's too hot to fly."

Hot air is less dense than cold, negatively affecting performance. The takeoff roll will be longer and the climb more shallow, and in very hot weather a plane may no longer meet the safety margins for a particular runway—such as climb gradient parameters and the distance needed to stop if takeoff is aborted. It's nothing so over-the-top as "unable to fly." Pilots and tech staff grapple with the data and a maximum takeoff weight is determined. Going a short distance with limited fuel, there won't be a problem, but with full gas and payload a reduction might be called for, meaning cargo or people must be bumped.

Some planes also have absolute operating temperatures stipulated in their manuals. At a certain threshold aerodynamic penalties become excessive and components begin to overheat. These limits tend to be quite high, usually around 50 degrees C (122 degrees F), but once in a while—maybe in Delhi in July—flights will be grounded outright.

As it works for temperature, it works for altitude. The higher you climb, the thinner the atmosphere, degrading aerodynamic efficiency and output of the engines. Even at maximum weight a plane might perform just fine from Honolulu, which sits at sea level, but will not behave with the same gusto at 35,000 feet. A flight may have to "step climb" its way to the most fuel efficient altitude, the restriction predicated not only on the physical ability to reach an altitude, but maintaining applicable stall buffer margins once it gets there. All of this is calculated by the crew, and is another reason pilots think of fuel in terms of pounds, not gallons.

Mexico City sits at 7,400 feet and is a great candidate for a payload hit, and I'll always remember a takeoff I once endured as a passenger on a 727 out of Cuzco, Peru, in the early 1990s. At 11,000 feet, Cuzco's airport is higher than the max *cruising* altitude of most private aircraft. We rolled and rolled and rolled until the plane at last, reluctantly, gave itself to that rarefied mountain air.

If ever you're wondering why South African Airways' New York-Johannesburg flight, one of world's longest *(see longest flights, page 260)*, only goes nonstop in one direction, this is part of the reason. The eastbound leg from JFK takes advantage of a long runway at sea level. Coming the other direction, Johannesburg's elevation entails a sanction, so the plane calls for fuel in Dakar or Cape Verde. Johannesburg is about the altitude of Denver. Most flights from Denver are not restricted, you'll say. Actually, they are. Because they are not, as in South Africa's case, attempting to travel 8,000 miles with full fuel, penalties aren't liable to apply.

Why do some planes leave those white trails in the sky?

Contrails are formed when humid jet exhaust condenses into ice crystals in the cold, dry, upper-level air, not unlike the fog that results when you exhale on a cold day. In other words, contrails are clouds. Water vapor, strange as it might sound, is a by-product of the combustion within jet engines, which is where the humidity comes from. Whether or not a contrail forms depends on atmospheric makeup—mainly temperature and something known as vapor pressure.

Aircraft leaving contrails are generally at very high altitudes. I've been watching contrails over Boston since childhood—a common sight directly above the city, especially in late afternoons and always in the same northeast-southwest alignment. The majority of these white lines belong to jets operating between Europe and New York. Every day, dozens of flights arrive and depart Kennedy and Newark airports, and their transatlantic routings shepherd them over Boston.

The environmental impact of contrails is the subject of study and debate. While you might be tempted to marvel at the innocuous beauty of these mile-high etchings, remember that there's more to jet exhaust than moisture. Although use of fossil fuels by commercial aviation hovers around 5 percent worldwide, the injection of pollutants directly into the upper troposphere is potentially more harmful than their amounts would insinuate. Emissions include not just water vapor, but carbon dioxide, nitrogen oxides, soot, and sulfate particles. Some of these react with the atmosphere to increase levels of ozone.

Separately, experts contend that the presence of contrails propagates the development of high, thin (cirrus) overcast clouds. Clouds breed clouds, you could say, and cirrus cover has increased by 20 percent in certain traffic corridors, which in turn influences temperature and precipitation. The journal *Nature* published a report confirming this. Beneath areas with the highest contrail concentrations, diurnal temperature fluctuations are greater than one degree below normal. What gave researchers a control group of unadulterated sky was the grounding of air traffic after September 11, 2001.

There's also the ongoing conspiracy theory claiming that some contrails are, in fact, noxious chemicals being sprayed by the military for purposes unknown. Some have drawn a connection between contrail presence—though in this case they are "chemtrails"—and illness in certain communities. The vast online docket of photographs and eyewitness accounts does have a certain UFO-sightings tinge to it. If the idea sounds particularly cuckoo, I'll mention that otherwise reasonable and skeptical people have taken to believing that *something* is going on, which is often a first sign that it is. That something, however, is probably no more villainous than standard military aircraft on maneuvers, albeit classified ones. If you live beneath one of these chemtrail-prone zones I'd recommend a good telephoto lens to identify what kinds of aircraft are involved. For the rest of us around major cities, all it takes is a decent pair of binoculars to realize the culprit is usually Lufthansa or Delta, and not some shadowy CIA spy plane.

NASA's space shuttle looks to be a sort of half-plane, half-spaceship hybrid. How would you compare the shuttle to an airplane, and astronauts to pilots?

In the sequel to Kubrick's *2001*, there's a scene where a TV is playing a commercial. Look closely and you'll notice it's an ad from Pan Am, hawking service not to São Paolo or Sydney, but into space aboard a ship that looks uncannily like NASA's shuttle. Clever, but Pan Am, transportation utopians that they were, really *did* presell a batch of tickets for proposed routes into orbit (think of the frequent flyer miles). And NASA, another group of visionaries, was eager to boast that its shuttle could and would make it possible. The Final Frontier as commercial promise, something greater than a tool of Cold War competition and a backdrop for extraterrestrial golf.

As happens, things evolved more slowly and more expensively than the dreamers hoped it might. But NASA's shuttle, inevitably restricted to missions of quasi-governmental nature, was built and flew successfully. Its liftoffs and landings grew so routine that the explosion of *Columbia* over Texas left millions of people thinking, "I didn't even know it was up there." But what *is* this thing—spaceship or airplane?

The shuttle was designed precisely as both. It goes straight up, just like the big old Saturns that carried the lunar landers, bolted to a tripod of rockets. But then it comes home again, as a *glider* for Chrissakes. And we can see the shuttle driver as a kind of transcendent superpilot, a meta-Yeager embodying some Ultimate Stuff. Not all crewmembers are qualified to steer the vehicle toward its landing spots in Florida or California, and those who carry such credentials are, well, pilots, traditionally top-rung flyers who cut their teeth in armed forces fighters. They sit before a console and joystick not at all dissimilar from those on a widebody jet.

I remember the day in August 1977, when I was in sixth grade and the prototype *Enterprise* made the shuttle's public debut. Fittingly, perhaps, the maiden voyage was strictly within the confines of gravity and atmosphere. *Enterprise* was but an airplane, released from a perch atop a Boeing 747 from where it would do nothing more elaborate than bank gently and glide to a stop in the Mojave Desert.

Watching that event unfold, I don't know what engrossed me more—the former American Airlines jumbo jet that carried the thing, or the piggybacked shuttle itself, which could have been described derisively as "about the size of a DC-9." There was a not-so-subtle allegory to the image—the iconic 747, like a mother bird, teaching its precocious chick to fly.

With allegories and images in mind, which works and forms of art do you think best evoke the spirit of aviation (whatever that is, exactly)?

Air travel is such a visual thing. Take a look some time at the famous photograph of the Wright Brothers' first flight in 1903. The image, captured by bystander John T. Daniels and since reproduced millions of times, is about the most beautiful photograph in all of twentieth-century iconography. Daniels had been put in charge of a cloth-draped 5 × 7 glass plate camera stuck into Outer

Banks sand by Orville Wright. He was instructed to squeeze the shutter bulb if "anything interesting" happened. The camera was aimed at the space of sky—if a dozen feet of altitude can be called such—where, if things went right, their plane, the *Flyer*, would emerge in its first moment of flight.

Things did go right. The contraption rose into view and Daniels squeezed the bulb. We see Orville, visible as a black slab, more at the mercy of the plane than controlling it. Beneath him Wilbur keeps pace, as if to capture or tame the strange machine should it decide to flail or aim for the ground. You cannot see their faces; much of the photo's beauty is not needing to. It is, at once, the most richly promising and bottomlessly lonely image. All the potential of flight encapsulated in that shutter snap; yet we see, at heart, two eager brothers in a seemingly empty world, one flying, the other watching him. We see centuries' worth of imagination brought to a bleak, almost completely anonymous fruition. Which is probably how it works—how it *has* to work—with many of history's more pivotal moments. This one, though, we've got on film.

With popular culture, I figure movies are the place to find the most meaningful and impressionistic tributes. One might parallel the 1950s dawn of the Jet Age with the realized potential of Hollywood—the turbine and Cinemascope as archetypal tools of promise. Decades later there's still a cordial symbiosis at work: a lot of movies are shown on airplanes, and airplanes are shown in a lot of movies.

The crash plot is the easy and obvious device, but although we might theorize what part of the shattered fuselage those Uruguayan rugby players (*Survive*, 1976, later remade as *Alive*) used as an abattoir when preparing their deceased teammates for consumption, the most thoughtful moments are when planes appear *incidentally*: the requisite farewell airport scene (always departing, never arriving); the propeller plane dropping the spy in some godforsaken battle zone, or taking the ambassador and his family away from one; the beauty of the B-52's tail snared along the riverbank in *Apocalypse Now*; the Polish jetliners roaring in the background of Krzysztof Kieslowski's *Decalog, Part IV*. For most of us, airplanes are a means to an end, and often enough the vessels of whatever exciting, ruinous, or otherwise life-changing journeys we tend to embark on. The furtive glimpses portray them best, far more evocatively than any blockbuster disaster script.

When it comes to music, I think of a United Airlines TV ad that ran briefly in the mid 1990s—a plug for their new Latin American destinations. The commercial starred a parrot, who proceeds to peck out several seconds of George Gershwin's "Rhapsody in Blue" on a piano. "Rhapsody" was United's corporate theme for several years, always a stirring accompaniment to the parting shot of a 777 set against the sky.

The Boeing family seems more musically inclined than most, and I know of at least three songs mentioning 747s, though we shouldn't forget the late Joe Strummer's reference to the Douglas DC-10 in the Clash's "Spanish Bombs." Somehow the Airbus brand doesn't lend itself lyrically, though Kinito Mendez, a merengue songwriter, paid a sadly foreboding tribute to the A300 with "El

Avion," in 1996. "How joyful it could be to go on flight 587," sings Mendez, immortalizing American Airlines' popular morning non-stop between New York and Santo Domingo. Flight 587 was well known among the city's Dominicans, familiar as any local bus. Five years after "El Avion," this bus, an Airbus A300, crashed in a neighborhood of Queens *(see flight 587, page 203)*.

The *Columbia Granger's Index to Poetry* registers no fewer than twenty entries under "Airplanes," fourteen more for "Air Travel," and at least another five under "Airports." Names here don't include Smith, but do include Frost and Sandburg. You're hereby spared my own aeropoems, but among my favorites are "Tarmac" and "On an Airplane." Maybe it was the cockpit checklists that inspired me, free verse masterpieces that they are:

> *Stabilizer trim override, normal*
> *APU generator switch, off*
> *Isolation valve, closed.*
> *Autobrakes . . . maximum!*

2

Turbulence for Tyros: Windshear, Weather, and Elements of Unease

. . .

> *"I felt about the Concorde as one might feel about a beautiful*
> *girl walking into class on the first day of school: I had to get*
> *close to her somehow, whether we actually hooked up or not."*
> —JAMES KAPLAN, IN *THE AIRPORT*

It had never crashed.

That was the notable thing about Concorde, or at least the one statistic everybody seemed to know. And citing the plane's so-far perfect record was, maybe, a distraction for the citizens of Britain and France, a comforting mantra in light of the billions of dollars they contributed to the SST (supersonic transport) project, entirely government-funded, that began in 1962.

As it was, however, Concorde was no safer than any other

airliner. This was, after all, a meticulously maintained ship that made, on average, only one or two flights a day—oceanic crossings along familiar routes to familiar airports. By the time production ceased in 1979, ten years after the prototype first took flight, only twenty Concordes had ever been built. An accident-free resume was more the work of probability than engineering. Owing to characteristics well-known to its pilots—aerodynamic instabilities and a hard-to-tame nature—one suspects a proportionate number of Concordes might have resulted in a different reputation altogether.

Contrary to popular knowledge, Concorde was not the only, or even the first, supersonic transport. (And however pretentious it seems, you're not supposed to put "the" in front of its moniker, something only CNN's Christiane Amanpour, probably a frequent rider herself, ever got right on TV. Amanpour was known to hang around Air France's *L'Espace* lounge on her days off, just for the free canapés.) The Soviets beat the Anglo and French engineers to the punch with the Tupolev Tu-144, a slightly larger lookalike that first flew on the last day of 1968. The race to produce the world's first faster-than-sound passenger plane even had its moments of intrigue and espionage, complete with the smuggling of Concorde specs into Russia inside toothpaste tubes.

Eager for glory, if apparently not glamour, the communists put their plane into revenue service on—and what can we call it but "the people's route"—the run from Moscow to Alma Ata, the now-capital of Kazakhstan. Such egalitarian deployment was something

Concorde would never see, despite its designers' dreams of a 400-plus fleet in the hands of the biggest airlines. Concorde would find its place as an anachronistic holdout—an Orient Express of the skies, a White Star Liner in a Carnival Cruise world of over-booked charters—and would stay there.

The Tupolev's career, punctuated by a disastrous crash at the 1973 Paris Air Show, was short-lived. On an intermittent schedule it would carry mostly freight. But Concorde, even in small numbers, its delta-winged profile instantly recognizable, became a star. Its haughtily graceful outline—and fares—express refinement and privilege, just as the industry was vectoring into the fury of deregulation. It was *international*, in a sexy, James Bond kind of way. The sleek superbird, with its hydraulically adjustable nose (for visibility during takeoffs and landings), was a kind of European emissary, an ambassador of aesthetic and technological triumph.

Sort of. The craft's wing may have been a superbly sculpted trophy of aerodynamic prowess, but the inevitable product of pushing an airliner—any airliner—across the Mach 1 barrier, is a need for prodigious power and the kind of fuel burn normally seen only by NASA *(see aircraft speed, page 57)*. The thirst of Concorde's engines—an underwing foursome of afterburning turbojets, would not be economically justified in an era of rising fuel prices. On an average transatlantic crossing a Concorde carried approximately a ton of kerosene for each soul on board. And that's with every of its hundred seats taken. Around-the-world marketing tours organized by its builders, France's Aerospatiale and the British Aircraft

Corporation, coincided grimly with the OPEC embargo and the '70s petroleum crisis.

On January 21, 1976, inaugural day of scheduled passenger service, a Concorde lifted off from Heathrow headed for Bahrain, and another from Paris to Rio de Janeiro. But commercially it was already over. Massive operating costs, along with virulent opposition to the jet's propensity for spewing out noise and air pollution, weren't winning the favor of airlines. Sign-carrying protesters often greeted Concorde arrivals. The Port Authority of New York, wary of Concorde's sonic booming and bad temperament, refused to grant landing rights at JFK.

British Airways and Air France purport their Concordes made money, a dubious assertion considering they were *given* the aircraft for free, never sacrificing a pound or a franc for acquisition. As R.E.G. Davies, curator at the Smithsonian Air and Space Museum puts it, "Had the Concorde ever been profitable, the world would have beaten Emerson's proverbial pathway to the doors at Toulouse and Bristol."

Although sixteen airlines, including Pan Am, Continental, and TWA, held options for Concorde deliveries—some seventy-four in all—most were canceled. Nobody outside of the flag carriers of Britain and France ever came to own one. Braniff International, the eccentric carrier from Texas, was the only American airline ever to have its hands in the Concorde story. As part of a code-share partnership in 1979, it flew Concordes between Dallas and Dulles. The flights operated subsonically, and although crewed and registered by the U.S. airline, it never wore a Braniff livery.

Once the ban was lifted in New York, it settled into regularity over the North Atlantic—Paris and London to Kennedy and Washington Dulles. At Kennedy, British Airways always parked its Concorde at gate 1, closest to the interterminal road, giving those of us stuck in cabs or stuffed into shuttles a view of what we were missing. Banking in over the coast, its sharply curving span formed a distinct and suggestive hourglass. The downward-arcing wingtips, long slender neck, and raked fin gave it a strangely anthropomorphic poise.

Concorde evoked a lot of things—a bird, a woman's back, an origami crane—but it never looked *old*. Its longevity was not just a milestone of economic endurance, but a statement of art and industrial design. Form followed function to a sensual, timelessly attractive end. What else in civil aviation, a world of Airbuses and pretzels, carried such an aura, and could still appear modern forty years after its blueprints were first drawn up? *Attention*. That's what Concorde was about.

And, of course, it never crashed.

Not until July 25, 2000. That day at Charles de Gaulle Airport, an Air France Concorde readied for takeoff. This particular ship, registered as F-BTSC, mothballed for some time, was recently given an overhaul and pressed back into service. It was the same aircraft once borrowed for the filming of *Airport '79*, and had even shuttled Pope John Paul II. Today its manifest included a full complement of one hundred—a group of German tourists headed initially to New York, and from there to catch a cruise boat in Ecuador. It was a charter flight, not the regular departure.

As the plane accelerated along the runway, it struck an L-shaped piece of titanium debris. Investigators would determine this piece had fallen from a Continental Airlines DC-10 that had taken off for Houston. Upon impact, one of Concorde's tires burst violently. It did so in a manner, as British Airways captain Mike Bannister would explain to *Airways* magazine, "In which four different manufacturers say they haven't seen in forty years of aviation." A chain of highly improbable events was about to end the lives of all those aboard. Down amidst the undercarriage, Concorde was playing the lottery with fate, and its number, just as it might for a commuter plane headed to Dubuque, had suddenly come up.

With tremendous velocity, a large chunk of exploding tire slammed into the underside of the wing, inside which, as in the case of all large airplanes, were hundreds of thousands of pounds of jet fuel. The cell was not impaled by the tire, but the resultant shock wave caused the fuel itself to knock out a section of its own tank, and the highly volatile liquid began to pour out, catching fire before the plane broke ground. The rest was essentially unavoidable, the consuming plume of flame rendering the plane unflyable before finally it wobbled into a hotel in Gonesse, on the outskirts of Paris.

Questions arose about the design of the tires and fuel tanks, and a month after the crash European aviation authorities revoked Concorde's airworthiness certification. Many saw the grounding as the end of Concorde altogether. "Despite the world's longtime fascination with the supersonic Concorde, its presence may come to a swift end," reported Diane Seo in Salon.com.

Both British Airways and Air France predicted differently.

Even after the attacks of 2001. In the post-attack turbulence, when reintroduction of a fuel-guzzling, technologically obsolete airplane seemed the last thing a reeling industry had use for, they pressed forward with reintroduction plans.

The plane was modified with high-tech Michelin tires and Kevlar-protected fuel bays. British Airways also revamped the interior, employing lighter-weight materials to offset additional weight imposed by the safety enhancements. Included in the plans were new seats and lavishly outfitted lavatories. Total investment in the refurb ran about $42 million at BA alone, split about halfway between the technical and cabin upgrades. Air France began airborne proving runs six months after the crash. BA commenced supersonic evaluations from Heathrow on September 11. Undaunted by the fallout of other occurrences that day, the testing continued at both companies.

And in November 2001, with two gleaming examples parked needle-nose to needle-nose in a ceremony at Kennedy Airport, British Airways and Air France officially resumed commercial Concorde flying. It was a dignified and defiant statement during tough times aloft, a glimmer of optimism for a throttled and nervous industry.

The plane's niche, after all—an intercontinental limousine for sheiks, tycoons, and film stars—was perhaps not so easily discouraged by current events as the noontime departure to Orlando. It's one of those "If you have to ask" things when it comes to the fare. Sometimes you came across ads in *Smithsonian* or the *New Yorker* for one of the airplane's yearly round-the-world charters—luxurious, multistop junkets at some absolutely ghastly price. A gorgeous, adrenaline-inspiring novelty, but beyond the reach of mainstream travelers.

Too far beyond. Concorde's phoenix act was all very inspirational—and maybe that was the only point—but it was over in less than two years. High-yield traffic over the North Atlantic wasn't recovering, upkeep was painstaking, fuel costs were breaking the bank. At the end of May 2003, Air France made a last departure between Paris and JFK, then flew a ship to Washington for exhibit at the Smithsonian. BA penciled its own goodbye for the following autumn and sent an example to New York City for exhibit on a barge along the Hudson River.

Final call after a career marked with as much excess as romance—too much noise, too much money, too much gas. Whether a Concorde or two ends up in private hands or sticks around for the air-show circuit remains to be seen. Either way it retired honorably, resilient vestige of a more daring, more visionary time.

Turbulence scares me to death. Do I have reason to be afraid?

A pilot worries about turbulence the way a sailor might worry about the waves. Or maybe that's a lousy analogy, since far more boats are swamped in rough seas than planes are kicked from the air. But you get the idea.

There are different causes and kinds of turbulence, a phenomenon which is no less a part of the sky than clouds or wind. Turbulence *is* wind. There's nothing like a good strong jolt to remind a passenger that he or she is aloft and at the mercy of an aircraft, but it will not dislodge a wing or otherwise knock you from the sky. Planes are built with a career's worth of rough air in mind, and what may feel like a serious airborne pothole is probably nothing to the metal beneath your seat. An airframe—even an old one—can take a remarkable amount of punishment.

In the mind's eye of a rider in coach, the plane is plummeting, like a ship toppling over the crests of giant swells. In reality, vertical displacement is infrequently more than about fifty feet, and the plane will not be snatched away and stomped into the ground. Just as you don't suddenly grab the wheel in a white knuckle panic when your car drives over a gravel road, pilots don't sweat during in-flight bumpiness. People often will say, "Wow, what a bumpy approach that was," yet the pilot will have little recollection of it having been bumpy at all. Not because he's jaded, but because he accepts and understands rough air. A wind-whipped landing is nothing too tense on the flight deck. Airplanes are inherently stable, always wanting to return to their original spot in space, and the crew is not wrestling with the beast as much as riding it out.

That said, really strong turbulence—it is graded from "light" to "extreme"—has caused damage and injury. Such incidents are strikingly out of the ordinary, and the amount of jostling it takes to slam a person against a wall or ceiling is not the sort of stuff even veteran flyers have encountered.

Pilots use preflight weather reports, cockpit radar, visible atmospheric cues, and reports from other aircraft to determine where rough air lies and how best to avoid it. But turbulence is invisible and difficult to predict, especially the variety that strikes from clear, cloudless air.

On takeoff one day we were tossed around very suddenly. The captain told us we'd been hit by "wake turbulence." What is this and how dangerous is it?

Wake turbulence, occasionally euphemized as "jet wash," is a somewhat routine and usually benign phenomenon. But put away your notions about that fasten-your-seatbelt-there's-some-rough-air-ahead kind of chop that whirlpools your coffee or causes you to miss a stroke on your laptop. This is something different.

At the tip of a plane's wing, the high-pressure air beneath the wing converges with the lower-pressure air above it, propagating a kind of twin-pronged roil of air that trails behind the aircraft like an invisible wake from a ship. Two vortices, one from each wingtip, are spun away like sideways tornadoes. They begin a slow descent, diverging slightly as they sink. Picture two long, violent fingers protruding from the back of an airliner like a forked, hanging tail. The vortices are always there, but their strength is exacerbated under certain combinations of aircraft speed, weight, and pitch angle. When a plane is heavy and traveling at a slow speed, as would be the case just after takeoff, they become especially pronounced, with rotational velocities approaching 300 feet per second.

Atmospheric conditions, particularly wind, break apart or dissipate a vortex before it's encountered. Flying in windy, bumpy air can actually be one of the best conditions for avoiding one. Controllers separate aircraft as necessary, while pilots are trained in methods that put them out of harm's way.

Most of the time. Every pilot has, at one time or another, had a run-in with a wake, whether it be the short bump-and-roll of a dying vortex or a full-force wrestling match. They usually last, at the most, a few seconds, and as you'd expect smaller aircraft are much more vulnerable than larger ones. I remember a calm night, standing along a seawall in South Boston less than a mile from the asphalt of Logan International. Every arriving jet was followed about thirty seconds later by an eerie snapping of air that sounded as if a giant leather whip were being struck over the harbor. These were the sideways tornadoes, touching down around me. Another time, as the captain of a commuter plane landing at Philadelphia, my aircraft was knocked wildly just a few hundred feet above the ground. It felt like we'd hit some Grade 6 whitewater in a rubber raft. The culprit was a Boeing 757 that arrived a few minutes earlier. The 757, owing to aerodynamic idiosyncrasy, is known to produce a particularly virile wake.

Sometimes when landing or taking off, I see a long trail of mist coming from the wingtip. What is this?

See above. As air flows around a wing at high velocity, its temperature and pressure change. When moisture levels are high enough, this causes the cores of the aforementioned vortices to become visible, shooting from the wings as strands of instantly condensed vapor.

Moisture will condense around other spots too, such as the engine attachment pylons. You'll witness what appears to be a stream of white smoke pouring from the top of an engine during takeoff. This is actually water vapor caused by invisible currents around the pylon. Other times, the area just above the surface of the wing will suddenly flash into a white puff of localized cloud. Again, this is condensation brought on by the right combo of moisture, temp, and pressure.

What is windshear? And can it rip the wings off?

One of those buzzwords that scare the crap out of people, windshear is a sudden change in the direction and/or velocity of the wind. Remember that a plane's airspeed takes into account any existing headwind. If that velocity suddenly disappears or shifts to another direction, those knots are lost. It can happen vertically, horizontally, or both, as in the case of a microburst preceding a thunderstorm. A microburst is an intense, localized burst of air from a storm front. Think of it like an upside-down mushroom cloud. The potency of windshear runs the range of barely noticeable to potentially deadly. When airplanes are taking off or landing, they operate very close to their minimum allowable speeds, and encountering a strong shear is dangerous. At higher speeds it's not of such concern.

Fortunately, windshear has become easier to forecast, and as a rule it does not appear out of nowhere, flipping a plane upside down without warning. Conditions that propagate shear are generally predictable, and pilots are trained to avoid them. Windshear got a lot of press in the 1970s and 1980s when it was still a misunderstood phenomenon. The crash of Eastern flight 66 in New York in 1975 is considered the watershed accident after which experts began to study it more seriously. The last headline crash attributed to windshear was in Dallas in 1985.

This rip-the-wings-off business is something I can't begin to address. It's like asking if a wave can break a ship in half. Theoretically, yes. Practically speaking, no. In the case of windshear, pilots are not worried about losing wings, they are worried about losing *speed*.

Over the Atlantic in a 747 we heard a very loud bang, followed by a palpable vibration through the cabin. The captain informed us we'd suffered an "engine pop." A *what*?

In their attempts to put people at ease, pilots can oversimplify things to the point where people begin giggling instead of nodding. What he was talking about was a "compressor stall," a phenomenon where airflow through the engine is temporarily disrupted. The compressors of a jet or turboprop consist of a series of rotating airfoils, and if air stops flowing smoothly around these airfoils, or backflows between the sequential stages, your compressor is stalling. It *can* damage an engine, but chances are it won't.

Miscellaneous engine peculiarities, compressor stalls included, can sometimes put on a show, and the visuals and aurals that accompany them aren't always comforting. Aside from a loud bang, you might see a long tongue of flame shooting from the exhaust. Tough as it might be to accept, the engine is neither exploding nor on fire. This is the nature of a jet. Any time a jet is running, fuel is combusting, and certain anomalies will unleash this combustion rather boldly out the back. The stalling compressors of an Alaska Airlines 737 once made the news when, by chance, this burst of flame was captured by somebody's camcorder on the ground. The video was alarming, but the phenomenon effectively harmless.

When this sort of thing happens at the gate or during taxi, passengers have been known to initiate their own evacuations. One such panic took place aboard a Delta 757 in Tampa, Florida. When a "large glow of orange" was seen emanating from the plane's right engine, a stampede of frightened passengers made for the exits, refusing to heed flight attendant commands. Two people were seriously hurt and thirty others received minor injuries.

How is a plane pressurized, and why?

Without pressurization, there would not be enough oxygen to breathe. We could stray into definitions of things like "partial pressure," but we'll keep it easy: As you go higher the air thins, which is to say the amount of oxygen decreases. Pressurizing the cabin effectively squeezes the air back together, re-creating the more dense, oxygen-rich conditions found on the ground. Or close to it, as during cruise the atmosphere in a jet is actually kept a bit higher than sea level—approximately the pressure you'd find at 5,000 to 8,000 feet. Otherwise, imagine having to sit there with one of those masks strapped to your head. Moreover, it allows for a gradual equalization as you climb and descend, making the flight more gentle on the ears. Pressurization is maintained via air from the compressors in the engines and regulated through valves in the fuselage.

That's all there is to it. Something about the word "pressurization" makes people envision the upper altitudes as a kind of barometric hell. I've been asked, "If the plane wasn't pressurized, would my eyes pop out?" Cruising in an airplane is not the same as dropping to the Marianas Trench in a deep-sea diving bell. It has nothing to do with eyes popping out; it has to do with oxygen. The outside pressure at 30,000 feet is no different than it would be atop Mt. Everest, also at 30,000 feet. Breathing on Everest isn't easy, but I've never heard of a climber's body exploding. Ear and sinus discomfort is matter of course, but unlike a SCUBA scenario even the most rapid pressurization change will not give you the bends or kill you. Sea level atmospheric pressure is about 14.9 pounds per square inch. At cruise altitudes a ballpark figure is about 11 pounds per square inch. Even an instant descent to sea level wouldn't cause serious harm.

If a malfunction arises, tie on your mask and breathe normally, just as the flight attendants tell you. If it needs to, the crew will descend to a height where the masks aren't required. This will take only a few minutes, and there's more than enough supplemental oxygen to go around. The presence of those masks, I know, is a source of angst for many. Should they spring from the ceiling en masse, try to resist shrieking or falling into cardiac arrest. Even in a worst-case decompression, you've got time to get the plastic on. As far as I know there has never been a case of an airline passenger dying from a pressurization problem.

Directly, anyway. Cruising along, there's little inherent danger in terms of pressure per se, either inside or outside. The inherent danger is the *difference* between the two. A pressurized cabin is, if you'll let me make the kind of alarmingly suggestive analogy I hate making, like a toy balloon. Losing pressurization is not, by itself, deadly, and in some cases a plane could lose every last psi and it would hardly be noticed. What's potentially deadly is losing it explosively, with resultant forces damaging or destroying the plane. A bomb might cause this, as could breaches of the fuselage, bulkheads, or doors, as happened to a Turkish Airlines DC-10 in 1974 following a cargo hatch failure (later redesigned), and a Japan Airlines 747 after a bulkhead rupture (earlier faulty repair). Awful to consider, yes, but equivalent misfortunes have been pleasantly few.

One reason an airplane's cabin windows are small—and round—is to better withstand and disperse the forces of pressurization. (Their size and shape also best assimilate the bending and flexing of a fuselage in flight.) I know what you're imagining: a burst window and people being sucked through the hole, headfirst. Has this ever happened? To find out we'd have to dust off some seldomly touched books or give Google an electronic heart attack, which basically tells you not to bother worrying.

How much fuel does it take to fly me across the country?

Traveling between New York and San Francisco, a medium-sized transport like a Boeing 767—a common model for this route—will consume roughly 7,000 gallons of jet fuel. That's equivalent to a little less than a half mile per gallon. With 200 passengers that's thirty-two gallons per person, or nearly eighty miles per gallon per person, which sounds more impressive. If you're the type who likes calculators, further crunching reveals 0.014 gallons for each, as they're termed in the trade, seat-mile.

To get a sense of industry-wide economy, you'd have to cipher averages of per-flight occupancy (flights in the U.S. have been operating at about 71 percent capacity), per-hour fuel burn, and flight distance. In deference to critics, if jetting across the continent weren't such a practical endeavor, only a fraction of today's passengers would actually be doing it. Still, overall efficiency is far and away better than a sixteen-mile-per-gallon SUV.

As for emissions, commercial aviation accounts for less than 5 percent of worldwide fossil fuel use. Not fully understood, however, are the impacts of chemically laden contrails and whether jet exhaust, injected directly into the upper troposphere, is uniquely harmful. At least one hydrogen fuel cell engine has undergone testing on a light plane, though I don't foresee hydrogen becoming status quo any quicker than it will for cars. It will take serious efforts and incentives from the government to make this happen, and the current political climate is not exactly warm, to make an ironic metaphor, to such changes.

I've been on flights where we circled for an hour before landing. How much fuel is on board, and is extra carried for these situations? Do airlines cheat to save money?

If you're impressed by big numbers, you'll be grabbing for the highlighter when you find out a 747 tops off its tanks at just over 45,000 total gallons. It takes about 11,000 to fill a 757, or 6,000 for a 737 or A320. A fifty-seater with propellers might hold less than a thousand gallons. Paltry in comparison, but still enough to drive your car from New York to California six times. Fuel is stored in the wings, in the center fuselage, and even in the tail or horizontal stabilizers. The cargo jet I used to fly had eight separate tanks, and much of my job was moving fuel around to keep them balanced.

Flights rarely depart with full tanks, as lugging around excess tonnage is expensive and impractical. Loads are ascertained according to regulation and subject to weather, traffic, and other variables. The regulations are intricate, differing between domestic and international operations, but the U.S. domestic rule is a good indicator of how conservatively things work: There must always be enough fuel to carry a plane to its intended destination, then to its designated alternate airport(s), and *then* for a minimum of forty-five minutes. Sometimes two or more alternates have to be filed in a flight plan (another batch of rules), upping the total accordingly. If delays or holding patterns are expected, even more is added.

The fuel portion of the preflight paperwork can be pages long and includes a detailed breakdown of anticipated burn. Amounts are cross-checked as waypoints are passed. Although dispatchers and planners devise the figures, pilots have the final say and can always request extra. Carrying surplus fuel costs money, but not nearly as much as the hassle of diverting.

Or crashing. Considering all of the above, the idea of running the tanks dry would seem far-fetched, yet fuel depletion accidents have occurred. To explain how, exactly, would entail pages of boring (for both of us) analysis, which I choose to withhold, but suffice it to say it's a little more complicated than a half-asleep copilot tapping a gauge and going, "Holy shit, we're almost out of gas." If you're a techie type, the Web can furnish in-depth explanations.

A couple of keywords to start with are Air Canada and Air Transat. A 767 belonging to the former and an A330 of the latter, a Canadian charter airline, had starring roles in the most recent out-of-gas embarrassments. Maybe it's a Canada thing. Air Transat's incident stemmed from mechanical trouble, while Air Canada's was principally human error, including a litres-to-gallons foul-up. In both cases crews managed to glide to a landing with no casualties. A bizarre chain of mistakes found a United DC-8 gliding into trees near Portland, Oregon, in 1978, and an Avianca 707 crashed on Long Island in 1990 after a series of arrival delays at JFK. Going back even earlier, a DC-9 once ditched near St. Croix, and in 1963 an Aeroflot jet glided into the Neva near Leningrad. Commercial jet travel in the '60s Soviet Union wasn't exactly state-of-the-art, so it's tempting to ignore that one entirely. In any case the plane remained floating and everybody escaped *(see water landings, page 200)*.

A half dozen blemishes over four decades? Compute those odds next time you're doing the rounds in a holding pattern and it'll help you relax.

Planes sometimes jettison fuel. Is this done to lighten the load for landing? Sometimes you can see it pouring from the wingtips.

Well-intended (or otherwise) people occasionally complain to authorities about visible streams of jet fuel trailing behind airplanes low to the ground. What they're witnessing are the wingtip vortices—spiraling trails of condensation spun from the wingtips by aerodynamic forces *(see wakes, page 46)*. You will sooner see an airliner spitting out bags of hundred-dollar bills than throwing away gas for no good reason. Under no circumstances do crews dump fuel unless during serious operational anomalies. And then, yes, it's to lighten the load.

With larger planes, maximum weight for takeoff is often greater than the one for landing. True for a few reasons, the obvious one being that touching down puts higher stresses on an airframe than taking off. Normally the suitable tonnage will be burned away en route—to the tune of hundreds of thousands of pounds on multihour legs. Now, let's say something happens soon after takeoff and a plane must return to the airport. Rather than tossing passengers or cargo overboard, it will jettison fuel through plumbing in the wings. I once had to dispose of more than 100,000 pounds this way over northern Maine, a procedure that took many minutes and afforded me a lavish night's stay at the Bangor airport Hilton.

Unless the trouble is urgent, dumping takes place at high enough altitudes where the kerosene mists and dissipates long before reaching the ground, and no, engine exhaust will not set the discharge aflame. In low-altitude emergencies this might not be possible, and hastily discarded jet fuel has been known to stink up neighborhoods from time to time. When it's do-or-die, a crew may forego dumping altogether and elect for an overweight landing.

Know that a plane dumping fuel and executing a precautionary return is not necessarily one in the throes of an emergency. Although "emergency landing" is used generically by passengers and press, to crews it's a very specific and rarely uttered term. Many, if not most, precautionary landings are not emergencies. And even when they are, a declaration of emergency is simply the best way to ensure sprightly handling by air traffic control. Don't let the crash trucks scare you; report a missing soda from the galley and the fire engines will likely be summoned.

It seems 757s always reach their destination more quickly. Should I look for a specific plane to get me to my destination faster? And when a flight departs late, why not simply pour on the coals to make up time?

Most jets cruise at roughly the same speed, give or take, indicated at higher altitudes by Mach number. Mach is the speed of sound (Ernst Mach is your man), and Mach *number* is a percentage of that speed. On a thirteen-hour journey between New York and Tokyo, the difference between, say, .84 Mach and .88 Mach would be relevant, but on short-hauls it's not worth worrying about. Assigned routings and air traffic are the determining factors.

Whether battling headwinds or delays, crews usually adhere to predetermined speeds to avoid messing with economy. "Pouring on the coals" burns fuel disproportionately to the amount of time it saves, and loads are sometimes planned under fairly tight constraints.

The border between subsonic and supersonic, near which most planes cruise, is not an aerodynamic triviality. In a poor man's version of Einstein's speed of light conundrum, required energy increases dramatically as you near the threshold. Though not an outright obstacle of physics, it's a huge pain in the wallet. To leave the sound barrier behind, a completely different wing is required and fuel use soars. That a Concorde looked and flew vastly different from a 747 was more than a quirk of design, as were its ghastly operating costs. For this reason, despite all the other technological advances we've seen, the cruising speeds of commercial jets have not really changed since their inception. If anything, the twenty-first-century airliner travels slightly more *slowly* than those of thirty years ago.

What happens when lightning hits an airplane? (Or maybe I don't want to know.)

Planes are hit by lightning more frequently than you might expect, and are designed accordingly. The energy does not travel through the cabin electrocuting the passengers; it is discharged overboard, partly through discharge wicks along the trailing edges of the wings and tail, nine times in ten leaving little or no evidence of the strike itself.

Once in a while there's damage or upset, most commonly to the plane's electrical systems. In 1963 lightning caused a wing explosion aboard a Pan Am 707 over Maryland. Afterwards, the FAA decided to enforce several protective measures, including fuel tank modifications and the installation of discharge wicks aboard all aircraft. That was more than forty years ago and I know of no other lightning disasters to date.

You can't have lightning without thunder, and using a plane's radar units, along with help from air traffic control, pilots avoid thunderheads the way ships avoid icebergs. Weather, though, can be sneaky, and smaller cumulonimbus are tough to detect. In 1993 I was captaining a flight between Halifax, Nova Scotia, and Boston, when lightning from a small embedded cell got us on the nose. What we felt and heard was little more than a dull thud. No warning lights flashed, no generators tripped off-line. Our conversation went:

"What was that?"
[Shrug]
"Lightning?"
"I don't know."

Mechanics would later find a black smudge not far from the cockpit windshield.

What happens if a bird hits a plane? Can it cause a plane to crash?

I've never considered the idea of birds hitting planes, and examples of ornithological suicide are undocumented. But you never know. As for planes hitting birds, that's another story. Bird strikes happen from time to time, and unless you're talking from the bird's point of view the damage tends to be minor or nonexistent.

In rare instances, though, it's serious. A military 707 crashed in Alaska after striking a formation of geese, and more recently a TWA 767 suffered an uncontained engine failure during takeoff from Tel Aviv after ingesting a gull. Birds don't "clog" an engine, but can bend or fracture the fan or compressor blades, causing power loss or failure. Airframes, including windshields and powerplants, are tested for bird resistance, while at airports, especially those along the coast, everything from shotguns to border collies are used to keep populations at bay. Birds are one of the reasons planes, at least in the USA, obey a 250-knot speed restriction below ten thousand feet.

One sometimes hears of icing after an accident. How can ice or snow cause a plane to crash?

During flight, ice can accumulate in different places—on wing edges, engine inlets, etc. Mostly it sticks to the thinner, lower profile areas, and not to larger expanses or the fuselage (a function of aerodynamics; let's not go there). This occurs during visible precipitation, or when suspended moisture sublimates directly. The monster here isn't the weight of the frozen material, but the way it changes the contouring of the airfoils. Even a quarter-inch ridge can wreak havoc—highly important during takeoff and landing when speed is slow and lift margins are thin.

On smaller planes, pneumatically inflated boots will break ice from the leading edges of the wings and stabilizers. On larger ones, air bled from the engine compressors heats wings and inlets. Windshields, together with various probes and sensors, are kept warm electrically. Deicing systems use redundant sources and are separated into independently functioning zones to keep a failure from affecting the entire plane.

Sitting at the terminal, an aircraft collects precipitation the same way your car does—via snowfall, sleet, freezing rain, or frost. Thanks to supercooled fuel in the wings, frost can form insidiously even with temperatures above freezing. Planes are scouted for ice before departing, and an airline's preflight deicing checklist can take up several pages of a pilot's manual. The delicious-looking spray (apricot-strawberry) used for ground deicing is a heated combination of glycol alcohol and water. It removes existing material and prevents the buildup of more. Different mixtures, varying in temperature and viscosity, are applied for different conditions. How long a plane is good for follows something called "holdover time."

Deicing fluid is collected and recycled, but at five dollars per gallon airlines loathe snowstorms almost as much as strikes, wars, and recessions. When handling and storage costs are considered, relieving a single jet of unwanted winter white can cost tens of thousands of dollars. Making a messy situation worse, glycol is toxic. What does our deicing future look like? It looks like a hangar—like the pioneering facility built at Newark by Continental, where planes are steered through enclosures that melt away ice using powerful infrared lamps instead of fluid.

I can't cite any cases of a jetliner going down from inflight icing, but in 1994 American Eagle flight 4184, an ATR turboprop, crashed out of a holding pattern over Illinois, killing everybody on board. The high-tech ATR is not the most aerodynamically robust of planes, and an ice ridge forward of the ailerons threw the wings into an unrecoverable stupor. This and earlier nonfatal incidents touched off a furor about whether the plane's maker, a French and Italian partnership, knew of flaws beforehand. Either way, the ATR's deicing system was redesigned. Of a handful of ice-related takeoff accidents, most notorious was the one involving an Air Florida 737 at Washington, D.C., in 1982. In addition to buildup on the wings, frozen-over probes gave a faulty, less-than-actual thrust reading after the crew failed to run the engine anti-ice system.

Are the contents of airplane toilets jettisoned during flight? Haven't there been reports of lavatory refuse falling on people?

Several years back I was on a train going from Kota Bharu, Malaysia, into Thailand, when I stepped into the rest room and lifted the toilet seat. I was presented with a mesmerizing view of gravel, dirt, and railroad ties, all passing rapidly beneath me. My *pinasse* trip up the Niger featured more or less the same thing. Those who've traveled around will know what I'm talking about, and maybe it's people like us who get these myths off and running.

A man in Santa Cruz, California, won a $3,000 suit against an airline when two pieces of "blue ice" came crashing like neon meteorites through the skylight of his boat. This was not the result of a couple of pilots prankishly reliving their combat days. What happened was a leak, extending from the toilet's exterior nozzle fitting, caused runoff to freeze, build, and then drop like an icicle. If you think that's bad, a 727 once suffered an engine separation after ingesting a frozen chunk of its own leaked toilet waste, inspiring the line, "When the shit hits the turbofan." (I just made that up, but I'll bet you anything somebody used it at the time.)

Your contributions to the airplane's plumbing, provided their composition isn't at violent odds with the blue fluid *(see The Exploding Toilet, page 111)*, are vacuumed into a tank and disposed of later. On busy multileg days, "We need lav service" is something a pilot—especially a regional pilot—says almost as much as "roger" when talking over the company frequency before landing. A truck then pulls up and drains out the contents. The driver's job is almost as lousy a job as the first officer's, but it pays better. Afterwards the man wheels around to the back of the airport and furtively offloads the waste in a ditch behind a parking lot.

In truth I don't know where it goes after that. Time to start a new urban legend.

Before boarding, we were told our flight was weight-restricted because of a malfunctioning system. Is it the crew's decision to take off when something important is not working?

Airplanes can depart with various inoperative components—usually nonessential equipment carried in duplicate or triplicate—in accordance with guidelines laid out in two thick manuals called the MEL (Minimum Equipment List) and CDL (Configuration Deviation List). Any component in these books is "deferrable," as we put it, so long as any outlined stipulations are met. These stipulations can be quite restrictive, depending on what's broken.

That's inviting some cynicism, but honestly the books are not contrived to allow airlines easy hand at flying around malfunctioning planes. Many things, as you'd hope, are not deferrable at all, and any malfunctioning item must be repaired in a set number of days or flight hours. All deferrals have to be documented and coordinated between the crew and maintenance personnel, a process that can entail a series of logbook notations and signatures. Above and beyond the deferral process, no respectable airline will pressure a crew to operate any flight. The final call, if you will, is the captain's, regardless of what the MEL or CDL allow.

Equipped with the latest diagnostic tools, some airplanes automatically transmit fault alerts en route, giving maintenance personnel early notice of malfunctions saving time at the destination. Advanced cockpits keep detailed software records of everything from internal engine temperatures to down-to-the-pound fuel burns. Data are downloaded—even from the ground while a plane is aloft—for scrutiny by technicians. Imagine it's like a black box for the guys with the wrenches and overalls. (Notice I say "technicians." At least one airline has banished the m-word altogether.)

When you watch a pilot do his walk-around check from the terminal, it doesn't seem a very in-depth inspection.

The walk-around inspection, while useful, is more of a supplemental, for-the-record sort of thing done in addition to more serious checks performed by the pilots and maintenance staff. It's essentially a superficial perusal, not a whole lot different from checking your oil, tires, and wipers before a road trip. The pilot follows a set pattern and a hundred items or more might be looked at. When finished he can entertain himself by reading the graffiti workers leave on the more grimy surfaces (VOTE NO is a common scribble around contract time).

The more technical preflight routine takes place out of view, in the cockpit. While you're bottlenecked at the mouth of the Jetway, the instruments and computers are being tested. Mechanics and pilots each have their procedures to run through prior to flight. And after too. Watch a plane dock and you might spot mechanics fanning out beneath it while another comes to the cockpit to consult with the crew and review the logbook.

I'm concerned about flying on older airplanes. Can I tell how far from retirement a plane is?

Retirement is an ambiguous term in the world of airplanes. Reassignment is the better one, as actual scrapping is fairly uncommon. It comes for various reasons, and age, strictly speaking, isn't always one of them. Planes are sold, traded, or mothballed not because they've become unsafe or are falling apart, but because they've become uneconomical. This may or may not be directly related to their date of construction.

Take the case of Delta and American, who chose to "retire" their McDonnell Douglas MD-11s, yet plan to hold on to older MD-80s and Boeing 767s for many years. Operators will speak of a particular model's "mission," one in which very fragile balances—tiny, shifting percentages of expenses and revenues—make the difference between red and black. Poor performance means quick exit to the sales block. To another carrier with different costs, routes, and needs, that same aircraft might be profitable.

When a China Airlines 747 crashed in 2002, the press jumped on the issue of aging airframes. The aircraft of the original "classic" series had been in service for twenty-two years, due for retirement in the next few weeks. Although no age-related failures immediately came to light, media coverage consistently invoked the 747's longevity (making cryptic reference to its ironically scheduled retirement) as a potential factor. "Why did they put this old plane in service?" asked a relative of three victims. Twenty-two years, after all, surely would find most aircraft in the scrapyard, right?

No, actually, and the flying public might be surprised to learn that a twenty-two-year-old 747 is hardly a geriatric jet. Commercial aircraft are built to last more or less indefinitely, which is one of the reasons they're so expensive.

Surprisingly—or maybe not—the U.S. majors rank *oldest* in a field of the largest fleets. Well past September 11, after which many chronologically-challenged jets were sent packing, it's not unusual to discover a twenty-five- or thirty-year-old example. The Asians and Europeans tend to fly the newest, and many of the most up-to-date fleets pop up in surprising places—Poland, the Czech Republic, Turkey. Youthfulness might be fostered by government subsidies (or outright ownership) in some nations, while in Europe tough antinoise restrictions essentially mandate newer planes. Frequently too it's the owner's progressiveness or pride. Lufthansa, Scandinavian (SAS), and Singapore are a few lauded airlines that make a point of quick turnover.

In America, exponentially larger fleets and enormous, model-specific inventories (maintenance supplies, ground equipment, etc.) make short-term renewals more burdensome. Most jets fall in the five-to-twelve-year-old range, though that number is going down. JetBlue surprised people by inaugurating service with brand-new Airbus A320s, a break from the assumption that new entrants and old airframes go hand-in-hand. A few others, like Southwest and Air-Tran, have been actively replacing older models.

The greater the total of hours in a jet's logbook, the more and better care it needs in the hangar. Older planes are rejuvenated with newer navigation systems and safety features, while the scrutiny of maintenance intensifies with every birthday. Though we needn't be reminded that perfection is impossible. In 1988 the upper fuselage of an Aloha Airlines 737 tore partially away during flight. Before the jet made a dramatic emergency landing, a flight attendant was killed and the living shit scared from everyone on board. Not only elderly, the jet had logged an incredibly high number of takeoffs and landings in a career spent island-hopping in Hawaii. Repeated pressurization cycles had weakened the inner structure. In 2002 the FAA implemented several new age-related inspections and record-keeping procedures for aircraft in service more than fourteen years. Corrosion, metal fatigue, and wiring concerns were among the impetus.

For the record, using 2003 information as this manuscript is prepared, the oldest average fleet among the largest worldwide contenders belongs to Northwest Airlines, with just over twenty birthdays per plane. American, Delta, and United all hover around ten. The oldest airplane in the world still carrying passengers with a major airline is a Northwest Airlines DC-9 built in September 1966, four months after I was born. Northwest still cares for several DC-9s that predate the Age of Aquarius. Should you feel any less at ease aboard these than a new A330 or 777? No. If your concerns rest with overhead luggage storage capacity or particle emissions from older-generation turbofans, go ahead and gripe. From a peace-of-mind standpoint there's little to be concerned with.

3

What Goes Up . . . Takeoffs, Landings, and the Mysterious Between

. . .

IDLEWILD, ROANOKE, AND TIMBUKTU TOO

Following the evolution of airport architecture, one notices a progression from bland utilitarianism to proud ideal and back again. The dawn of commercial flight gave us barns and wood-frame hangars, followed in the '30s by more exalted structures built with the spirit and permanence of railroad terminals (pay a visit some time to Lunken Field in Cincinnati). Then, as the number of passengers soared and airports required greater size and expandability, we saw the more strict, unimaginative deference to the lowest common denominators of cost control and ease of construction.

Such a statement is a tad disingenuous, as architectural language, of course, speaks to its time, and today's nondescript hallways and soot-stained girders were yesterday's stunning achievements. But somewhere along the way the airport ceased to exist as symbol or spectacle. Unfortunate, really, for as any lover of air travel will tell you: *It's the departure, stupid*.

At John F. Kennedy Airport, Eero Saarinen's 1962 TWA terminal is a modernist masterpiece and one of the best backdrops for revisiting a little Jet Age enchantment. Saarinen, a Finn whose other projects included the Gateway Arch in St. Louis and the sweepingly beautiful main terminal at Washington Dulles, described his TWA as "all one thing." The lobby is a fluid, unified sculpture of a space, futuristic yet firmly organic. It's a kind of Gaudi inversion, a sand-colored, carved-out atrium reminiscent of the caves of Turkish Cappadocia, overhung by a pair of cantilevered ceilings that rise from a central spine like huge wings. As did the spidery "Theme Building" at LAX, conceived around the same time, it became an nonconformist icon. Not necessarily because of any thumbprint novelty, but because it returned a sense of identity to the modern airport, a vitality that would lend itself in years to come to a host of facilities around the world.

In the mid 1990s I worked in that building, based there with the commuter affiliate of TWA. I'd sit in the second-story restaurant looking down into the lobby, at the gangs of kids in sandals, eyes locked on their copies of *Details* or *Spin* and waiting for final call to Tampa or Dallas or Tel Aviv. It was undersized and forlorn by then, plaintive and world-weary in that way only airports can be— greased and smeared by every nation and culture without ever having lifted its girders from the Jamaica Bay fill. Clutches of sparrows and starlings lived in the yellowed rafters and would swoop around grabbing up crumbs.

Unoccupied after TWA was subsumed by American Airlines, the structure's fate was arbitrated between preservationists and Port Authority bureaucrats. As those things tend to go, few were optimistic, and the demolition teams were readying their bulldozers. But thanks to efforts of the city's Municipal Arts Society, an agreement was reached that will leave the terminal not only standing, but rejuvenated as a showpiece for Kennedy's hip new hometown airline, JetBlue.

Meanwhile, if you'd like to see the world's largest stained-glass window, no need to invest in a ticket to Rome or Barcelona. Merely hop a ride on the candy-striped Port Authority bus over to American's Terminal 8.

The terminals at JFK, unlike most big airports, are unconnected and arranged in a mile-wide circle. When laid out half a century ago, the biz still rife with delusions of eternal eminence, the buildings were called "jewels in a necklace." It was still Idlewild Airport then, the strangely evocative name borrowed from a golf course on the original site. Just south of Kennedy's perimeter is the great marshy basin known as Jamaica Bay, whose islands comprise a wildlife refuge and something called the Gateway National Recreation Area, the northeast corner of which borders the runway complex. I once saw a pelican gliding low along a taxiway here.

It's hard to miss the enormous oval rooftop of what was once the Pan Am Worldport. Now it's a hub for Delta and renamed, in a gesture of almost sacrilegious ignominy, Terminal 3. This is the building where the Beatles declared themselves bigger than Jesus, arriving from London on flight 101. This is where Khruschev stepped from his Tupolev, where starlets waved from metal stairs pulled up to Constellations and DC-7s. Today it's just this old dirty building, an overworked, confounding warren of passageways and glass partitions. The ceiling hangs like a giant flying saucer, a Jet Age architectural fantasy, but the history, the *context*, is gone. The space is vapid, as if starving for the burst of a blue flashbulb, somebody signing autographs.

Kennedy might be the perennial loser in the minds of weary travelers, but I suppose one learns to love it the way Scorsese, who immortalized the place through the infamous Lufthansa heist in *Goodfellas*, loves New York itself, as a multiform world of grit, corruption, and beauty. For JFK is as comprehensive a melting pot as you'll find—a round (literally) little microcosm of *el mundo* itself—not to be outdone anywhere in America. I love seeing Sikhs, Moroccans, Colombians, Arab women with their faces covered, all in a frantic, teeming mingle while muscled Port Authority cops look on suspiciously. It's an illusion, of course, a foisted integration that lasts exactly until final call once again splinters the masses into their respective creeds and colors. But as the departure lobbies fill and the check-in lines swarm, it's a snapshot of multicultural nirvana that would make any campus radical weep with happiness.

Outside, the crazy colors of a hundred different airlines line the tarmac, pure exotica for an airplane nut. The inter-terminal bus says it all, its stops along the necklace so saturated with international carriers that the PA blares not the airline name itself (Malev), but the country it serves (Hungary). Ghana, Pakistan, South Africa. They're all here.

If you're still not inspired, drive across Queens to La Guardia, where you can savor the gleaming art deco doors of the Marine Air Terminal (1939), formerly the property of Pan Am and now directly adjacent to the Delta Shuttle. Inside the rotunda is a 360-degree mural and cutaway of an old Pan Am seaplane. The mural, *Flight*, is a 1952 work by artist James Brooks. As it traces the history of aviation from mythical to (then) modern, Icarus to flying boat, you may notice the painting's style is a less than shy nod at socialist realism. At the height of '50s McCarthyism, in a controversy not unlike that of Diego Rivera's infamous mural at Rockefeller Center, it was declared a gesture of socialist propaganda and obliterated with gray paint! Not until 1977 was it restored.

Which isn't to dwell too haughtily in the past. Some of the latest airport projects are among the most resplendent. With its latticework façade and giant horizontal louvers, San Francisco's new international terminal, largest in North America, is one dazzling example. Or, my favorite, British Airways' sublimely ultramodern World Cargo Centre at Heathrow.

Yet the more I see of our newest and more grandly-proclaimed facilities, the more they look the same and the more I'm convinced the evolution of airport design will not be complete until the Beverly Hills mall and terminal become virtually indistinguishable. Judging from what I saw recently in Dubai and Kuala Lumpur, that day is coming soon.

Dubai International, in the United Arab Emirates, is the busiest airport in the Middle East and home of aptly named Emirates, arguably one of our three or four best airlines. Almost a hundred carriers fly here, and sixteen million passengers come and go every year, a total expected to *double* by 2010.

If you ask me, DXB is clean, accommodating, and terribly overrated. The multistory Sheikh Rashid Terminal is a cross between an upscale shopping center and the lobby of a luxury hotel, overhung by a plaster façade of caravansary-style archways and a chintzy mural of Arabian horses. It's a Trumpy, Vegas brand of opulence that's more or less in tune with the gold-and-glass glitz that personifies this wealthy Gulf state.

Kuala Lumpur International, in Malaysia, was completed in 1998. One of several new Asian megaprojects, it sits about an hour south of the capital, in the heart of Malaysia's high-tech "multimedia supercorridor." With 25,000 acres, KUL is one of the most expansive airports and features the world's tallest control tower. It's a clean, spacious, well-ordered place with its own in-terminal rainforest. Like Kuala Lumpur itself the atmosphere is surprisingly lush and tropical. And as in every other big new airport, passengers parade through corridor after corridor of shops bursting with expensive clothes, jewelry, perfumes, electronics, and chocolate. We're led to believe there's not an air traveler alive who isn't desperate for a last-minute designer bag, diamond necklace, or a $350 pen from Mont Blanc.

KUL's star is the "Ekspres" train running directly from the

main lobby to downtown's KL Sentral station. Patrons of Malaysia Airlines, Cathay Pacific, or Royal Brunei can check luggage and receive seat assignments at the in-city train platform, a perk that earns the station its own three-letter code—XKL.

On a much smaller scale, how many of you have ever seen Roanoke Regional Airport in west-central Virginia? Brick archways and exposed girders offer the look and personality of a renovated Blue Ridge warehouse. It's a faux, Applebee's style of down-home, but the effect is disarmingly comfortable. Much in the way Baltimore's Camden Yards works for baseball, Roanoke's retro works for airports.

. . .

And if ever you've got some time to kill in the hinterlands of West Africa, do as I did recently and pay a visit to that jewel of Saharan excess, Aeroport de Tombouctou.

Your choice of Timbuktu, Timbuctoo, or the French Tombouctou, you'll find it in the anvil-shaped country of Mali, along a northern bend of the Niger with the colossal expanse of the Sahara just beyond. Although still one of the most famous places in the world, Timbuktu made its fortunes in the fifteenth-century salt trade, when it also was a center of Islamic intellectualism. Today it exists as an oddly picturesque town hosting the occasional tourists who come to savor the accomplishment of having made it to a place synonymous with the middle of nowhere. And where there are tourists, there are airports.

Although I'd arrived by boat, I had a few spare hours one scorching afternoon and couldn't resist a visit. Posing as a *liaison d'avion*, "on assignment" of course, from "a major American magazine." Soliciting the company of local guide and aviation aficionado Aly Dicko, I hired a Land Rover for the five kilometer drive. The airport is on the town's southern outskirts, across the street from a bleak, treeless expanse that Dicko explains was once a camp for displaced members of the Bella tribe, slaves of the local, Bedouin-descended Tuaregs who dominate the Saharan regions of Mali.

I expected nothing more than a thatch covered shack—maybe with a few of those ubiquitous Malian goats pulling a sand-encrusted luggage cart—only to find something entirely different. The handsome terminal, designed by the international firm of Dar Al-Handasah, is a Sudanese-style building emulating the mud-built mosques found all over Mali. The interior, while cheerless, appears spacious and functional. There are separate areas for arrival and departure, a small shop, a bank of Western-style check-in counters, and a passport control station.

Along the northern edge of the building, a smoothly paved ramp leads to a 6,900-foot runway. Dicko points out a low, flat structure with a brown roof that he tells me is the "old" terminal. This building, which looks in perfect working condition, isn't unlike many of the small terminals you'll find in the American Midwest. It would be the envy of many third world airports, but in Timbuktu it's not even the nicest.

Everything seemed to be in place, save two things: people and airplanes. Not a single plane, military or civilian, public or private, was parked anywhere on the property. A glance through my binoculars revealed the control tower vacant as well. The effect was so eerily hushed one wondered if anybody had *ever* been there.

Mali might be one of the poorest nations on earth, but they've built this incongruous trophy in the middle of nowhere and apparently for nobody. You'll find this sporadically in certain corners of the globe—ill-afforded extravagance on behalf of commerce and tourists that never come. If you've ever been to the obscenely oversized airport in Mandalay, Burma, you'll know what I'm talking about.

"Three flights a week," Dicko tells me. This may or may not be accurate, but the particulars of Malian commercial aviation prove entirely elusive. The check-in kiosks are clean and modern, but there are no computers or airline logos. The closest I discover is a hand-stenciled AIR MALI in white paint on the front of a locked door, and a decal for something called "African Airlines." (The national carrier, Air Mali—which over the years earned the nickname "Air Maybe"—has been around in one form or another since about 1965.) Dicko says occasional charters arrive directly from France, the country's old landlord, and the runway length and facilities suggest this is possible.

Getting to Mali from America is surprisingly simple, except you'll be landing in the capital, Bamako, not Timbuktu. Until recently you could fly directly from New York to most of West Africa on the notoriously . . . let's just call them colorful, Air Afrique, transferring at Dakar. For me it was Air France, and a connection at Charles de

Gaulle, where a security screener confiscated my mosquito repellent, protesting, "The gas! The gas!" when I demanded it back.

Why do planes take off and land into the wind?

Recall how a plane stays in the air and imagine there's a fifteen-knot headwind pointing down a particular runway. Well, if a plane's intended takeoff or landing speed is 120 knots, then fifteen of those already are taken care of.

For the sake of argument, imagine there's a hurricane blowing at 200 knots and you tow a 757 from the hangar and turn it toward the storm. Tethered in place, the plane could lift off and "fly," just as it would to Denver. What would the airspeed gauges read? Two-hundred knots, even as it hovered motionless vis-à-vis the pavement. The plane does not care how fast, or in what direction, it moves over the ground, only how fast it moves *through the air*. That's the difference between airspeed and groundspeed. Up in a two-seater you can point your nose into a strong wind, slow the craft as much as possible, and sure enough you'll drift backwards like a kite.

For traffic management or to avoid noisy neighborhood over-flights, into-the-wind operations aren't always possible, and you're stuck with a crosswind or tailwind. Tailwinds are meaning-less to airspeed, but will increase groundspeed; beneficial during cruise, but not much fun when taking off or landing. Racing down a runway, a plane will be pushed along, using up valuable real estate while actual flying speed—*airspeed*—is unaffected.

Allowable tailwinds for takeoff or landing are very low, around ten knots or so.

Can you explain how a plane takes off and why it bumps, jigs, and turns, sometimes at a high angle during the climbout?

The plane accelerates and reaches a predetermined speed. The pilots then rotate the aircraft to a specific angle and begin the climb. The distance along the runway at which this happens, as well as the power setting used to get there, is different for every occasion and is calculated beforehand. It depends not just on the weight of the plane itself, but temperature, wind, and other factors. After breaking ground, the pilots follow a "profile" of speeds and altitudes at which they retract the gear and flaps, reduce or increase angle, etc., all while turning to assigned headings and climbing to assigned altitudes. Because you're close to the ground and climbing at high power settings, the sensations of takeoff tend to be exaggerated.

If it seems takeoffs from certain airports are unusually hectic, chances are good the plane is following a noise abatement procedure on behalf of residents below. These require some of the most intensive profiles, with low altitude turns or steeper climbs.

Inherently, takeoff is the more critical point than landing. Here the airplane is making the transition from ground to flight, and its grip on the latter is much more tentative than when coming down. More passenger fingernails are probably chewed during landings, but in deference to the laws of inertia, gravity, and momentum, this anxiety is somewhat misplaced. If you insist on being nervous, liftoff is your moment.

During early climb, engine thrust is suddenly cut and it feels like the plane is suddenly falling. What is happening here? It seems like a poor time to ease back on thrust.

The thrust used for takeoff itself is, in the interests of safety and performance, more than enough, and so it's lessened once aloft to save wear on the engines and to keep from exceeding target speeds. Noise abatement procedures also play a role here. The plane is still climbing and is not decelerating nearly as much as it may feel. Despite the impressive roar of the engines and spine-straightening acceleration, airliners usually do *not* take off at full bore. Maximum thrust is used when conditions dictate (weight, runway length, and weather), but normally they don't, instead allowing a preordained thrust setting some degree below the available output. As with the climbout cutback, this saves engine life. Needed thrust is set by the crew and fine-tuned automatically as the plane accelerates.

What if, just at the second of liftoff, something happens?

Before every flight the particulars of weight, weather, and runway are juggled to ensure a safe takeoff. Even a dying engine should not cause havoc, as every airliner, including turboprops, is certified for takeoff with a powerplant quitting at the worst possible moment. That worst possible moment is known to pilots as V_1, referring to the speed at which discontinuing the takeoff is no longer an option. If you're intimidated by mathematical style symbols, think of it as "decision speed." Prior to V_1 safe stoppage is guaranteed, but after V_1 this isn't always true. If an emergency of any magnitude occurs beyond V_1, crews are trained to *continue the takeoff*, as per regulation planes must be capable of accelerating and climbing away, even with total failure of an engine.

This guarantee extends beyond the airport perimeter to account for buildings, mountains, TV antennae, and whatever else. For each airport—indeed each runway—data are computed to assure not only the ability to fly, but to avoid off-airport obstructions, even with a failed engine.

But what about prior to that V_1 point? If a takeoff is aborted, doesn't a full load guarantee we'll be crashing off the end of the runway?

When all the numbers are crunched, two things are assured: First, as detailed above, that a plane can safely climb away if an engine quits at the worst moment. Also, if takeoff is discontinued *up to that moment*, this same plane must be able to stop on the remaining pavement. This includes applicable penalties for ice, snow, or any other performance-altering peculiarities of a runway.

This is one of the reasons flights may be weight-restricted when using short runways. Not because the length is inadequate for takeoff, but because it's inadequate for an *aborted* takeoff. With V_1 as the index, the necessary distance on the "stop" side can often exceed that on the acceleration side.

Which isn't to say no plane has ever slammed on its brakes and gone skidding off the end. It happens from time to time, meaning very infrequently. To help the cause, modern airplanes are equipped with extremely sophisticated pilots *and* extremely sophisticated brakes.

A friend of mine was on a plane when a burst of fire came spurting from an engine during takeoff. The passengers began shouting and a flight attendant radioed the cockpit. The plane lifted off, then dropped to the ground and stopped.

This nicely illustrates some rather blatant PEF, or Passenger Embellishment Factor, the phenomenon that accompanies so many (usually second- or third-hand) accounts of dodgy takeoffs, aborted landings, near-misses, and so on. Earmark this page for the next time you're subject to a watercooler tale like this one. Though not a witness to the "burst of flame" and the alleged follow-up excitement, I have my hunches.

If a departure is discontinued for "engine trouble," that does not mean the engine was coming to pieces, blowing up, or even failing to run. Most always it's due to faulty RPM acceleration, not hitting a target value of torque or thrust, or some such technical, very non–life threatening irregularity. The above case sounds like a compressor stall, which is slightly more serious but nowhere near deadly *(see compressor stalls, page 49)*.

Regardless, this all would take place *before* liftoff. I can't accept an account of becoming airborne and then touching down again, especially if an engine problem was the culprit. Although it *has* happened, no pilot is trained this way. As we've gone over, airliners can safely take off and climb with a totally failed, for that matter flaming, engine. For this story to be true, the situation would've been excessively unusual.

Furthermore, flight attendants will not "radio the cockpit" (actually there's a phone) while barreling down the runway, and no pilot would answer such a call at or near takeoff speed.

Shortly after beginning to roll, takeoff was discontinued and we came to a stop. A minute or two later we restarted from the point we'd left off. I can't help wondering how much of the runway we'd already used. How did the pilots know enough remained?

Airplanes ordinarily take advantage of a runway's full length, and this includes returning to the threshold after any halted run. But at times this isn't practical or necessary. So-called "intersection departures" are used all the time in many places. The name refers to the point at which a taxiway enters onto a runway and from where planes will launch. A popular one is the "KK" (taxiway designator) takeoff from runway 31L at Kennedy International. Here, several thousand feet of asphalt are bypassed. Not to worry when 10,000 more remain.

It's not like the crew figures, "Yeah, this is probably enough room," and gives it a go. As already summarized, runway length must always be sufficient for an aborted takeoff. In this case a second one. If it seemed your crew was able to calculate rather quickly, this info can be processed by the folks backstage—dispatchers and flight planners—and relayed via computer or radio in a matter of seconds. Alternately, it's available in the tables and graphs of the cockpit performance manuals. Pilots on the cutting edge—at Jet-Blue, for one—consult their onboard laptops.

Just before touchdown, our flight powered up and aborted the landing. We banked around at severe angles, approached a second time, and landed. They told us the airport was attempting to squeeze out too many departures.

What you experienced was something so nonthreatening that the crew had mostly likely forgotten about it by the time they were waiting at the curb for the hotel shuttle. Now and then, for any of various reasons, spacing between airplanes falls below the minimums and a plane is told to execute the procedure you describe—to us it's called a go-around. It's troubling, though not surprising, that flyers are so put off by something so innocuous. Crews owe a more professionally soothing explanation than a folksy spiel about the tower trying to "squeeze out too many departures."

Having to go around does not, except in highly extraordinary circumstances, propose that you were close to hitting another aircraft. The limits are set for that reason—to keep you *away* from any jeopardizing encroachment. In 2003, of 339 runway incursions reported, the FAA deemed only three as having been "a significant risk for collision." Yet these events have a way of becoming, "We were just about to land, but another plane got in the way and we had to *zoooooom* over the top of it!"

A variant of the go-around, and spoken of somewhat interchangeably, is the "missed approach," whereby a plane pulls off the same maneuver for weather-related reasons. If, in the course of an instrument approach, visibility drops below a prescribed value, or the plane has not made visual contact with the runway upon reaching the minimum allowable altitude, the crew must climb away.

If the pilots aren't crackling over the PA to explain what's going on, don't construe the silence as concealment of some imminent disaster or near-miss. Go-arounds and missed approaches are the most work-intensive phases of any flight. The crew will be busy coordinating with air traffic control, resetting autoflight systems, dialing in altitudes, and headings, retracting flaps and gear.

The flying around at "severe angles" part is nothing more than some close-in maneuvering to rejoin the pattern. Chances are good you'll undergo an abrupt climb and a few sharp turns. Or else they just seem that way. Layperson guestimates of turns, climbs, and descents tend to run about double the actual values. Unless there's some desperate situation, aircraft will never exceed more than about 30 degrees of bank or 20 degrees of pitch. "Steep" banks and climbs are on the order of 25 and 15 degrees respectively. At 60 degrees you'd be pulling twice the load of gravity (2 g) and would struggle to lift your legs from the carpet. You've never been close to 60, or even 45 degrees in an airliner.

I notice a successive arrangement of signs along the edge of the runway. Each features a single digit, and they go in order: 8, 7, 6, 5, and so on.

This might be more incentive for passengers to keep their eyes on the newspaper instead of out the window, but yes, these indicate the distance remaining in thousands of feet. If you're departing on a 10,000 foot strip, expect to see a 4 or 5 zipping by as you leave the pavement. Naturally, this depends. During that departure from Cuzco years ago, I distinctly recall a 2 going past my window in a blur while the tires were still firmly on the ground. Don't fret, because if you're paying attention then you already know takeoffs are calculated to ensure enough room for stopping should the need arise. That's a bet I wouldn't have taken in Peru, by the way, but my experience there was about as envelope-pushing a scenario as exists.

Runway striping also can be used to measure distance, but this isn't visible from the cabin and I won't bore you with the meanings of the different stripes and bands. The signs, lights, and markings section of the Aeronautical Information Manual features twenty-seven pages of diagrams and explanations.

Our pilot told us we were taking off on runway 22 at La Guardia. Are there really twenty-two runways at the airport?

The numbers correspond to the runway's magnetic (compass) orientation. Picture a 360-degree circle. To figure out which way a runway is pointing, add a zero. Runway 22 is pointing 220 degrees, toward the southwest. The opposite end of the same strip would be designated 04, pointing 40 degrees, or northeasterly. The cardinals are 09, 18, 27 and 36. Therefore, one runway is actually *two* runways. Departing on 09, you'll be taking off into the sunrise; departing 27, you're headed directly westward. Both, however, are the same stretch of pavement.

An airport can have several runways aligned in all manner of geometry—triangles, perpendiculars, crisscrossing tic-tac-toe—or just one. Seen from above, Chicago's O'Hare looks like an aerial view of the Nazca Lines, with seven separate strips for a whopping fourteen total runways. By comparison, Tokyo's Narita operated for many years with only one. A common layout is that of two parallel strips, either side-by-side or with the terminal complex sitting between. You'll see this in places like Seattle, Charles de Gaulle, and London Gatwick. At Los Angeles and Atlanta, there are *two* sets of side-by-side pairs. Laid in parallel, runways are given a letter suffix of "L" or "R," designating left or right. Once in a while there's a center parallel using "C."

There's no standard length, which like the varying outfield fences of Major League baseball stadiums, adds some, er, character to certain airports. La Guardia and Washington National are known for short, unforgiving runways of about 7,000 feet. Runway 31L at JFK is more than twice that long, and for a while was a designated emergency landing strip for the space shuttle. Eleven thousand feet is a classic "long" runway. Excavated, paved, lighted, and instrumented for all-weather ops, a runway is a much more serious undertaking than slapping down asphalt and painting stripes on it.

The sixth runway at Denver International carried a tab of $165 million.

I live near a small-town airport, and one day a 767 diverted here after a maintenance problem. How could such a large plane land at such a small field?

Before getting into this, I should preface by reminding you that just as big airports can have unusually short runways, out-of-the-way airports can have surprisingly long ones. Don't be amazed if ever you see a 747 at Toledo or Columbus, Ohio, both with strips over 10,000 feet. Use by the military, among other things, play into an airport's runway prowess.

While many runways are categorically too short to accommodate larger planes, there is no standard distance required by any aircraft to take off or land. It is always different. Charts or databases are consulted to deduce maximum allowable weights for a given runway. Variables include not merely the end-to-end length, but wind, surface conditions, off-field obstructions, and potential emergency maneuvers.

Smaller airports with smaller runways are generally served by smaller planes, but this can be more a function of practicality and logistics than size, strictly speaking. While it's doubtful you'll ever see a 747 at Washington National or La Guardia, where the longest runway is a measly 7,000 feet, that's not to imply one couldn't land there. Rather, its payload—particularly its carriage of fuel—would be so restricted by, to phrase it one way, the proximity of Flushing

Bay as to render it economically unfeasible. Sometimes, if it helps fill a gap in an airline's timetable or augments capacity between certain cities, that's a hit worth taking. You'll find 767s operating out of La Guardia all the time. Could one take off for Hawaii with its tanks full? No.

Apart from all this, a big misconception is that the largest airplanes by nature require the longest runways. Not always true. The 747 was more than twice the tonnage of the plane it superceded, the 707, yet its takeoff and landing rolls were about the same. Large airliners generate enormous amounts of lift and whip up mammoth quantities of power. The leviathan A380 is designed to have a landing speed (about 140 knots) no different from the A320, a quarter of its size, and under most conditions will require *less* runway than a 747.

How does a plane find the runway during lousy weather? Those foggy landings always scare me.

The standard procedure for bad-weather approaches is, and has been for decades, something called the Instrument Landing System, or ILS. Essentially, a plane follows two guidance beams, one horizontal and one vertical. Transmitted from antennae on the ground, these guide an airplane along a descending path to the runway with close to unfailing accuracy. By centering the two beams in a kind of electronic crosshair, either manually or automatically (the autopilot flies and the pilots monitor), an airplane descends to a certain height—usually about 200 feet above the ground, though sometimes lower—at which the runway must be visible for landing.

Some ILS are certified for lower visibility approaches than others, and in certain cases zero-visibility landings are authorized *(see following questions)*. Runway visibility is measured using something called RVR (runway visual range), where a series of light-sensitive machines arrayed along the runway provides values in feet or meters.

GPS, while in general use for en route navigation, is still an incipient technology when it comes to bad-weather landings, and precision GPS approaches require the use of ground-based augmentation units to correct for small errors in satellite signals.

An article stated autopilot features are now so advanced they can land airplanes in bad weather on their own. Is this true?

Be aware that "autopilot" is a fairly euphemistic term. A plane's autoflight systems might consist of two or more autopilots, actually, and their various—and extremely complicated—computerized subfunctions.

Autoland, a subfunction of sophisticated automatic pilots, has been around for over three decades. The British-built de Havilland Trident was the first to have this capability, in 1967. A true, no-visibility automatic landing is exceptionally rare, but even in good weather a crew will occasionally execute one for practice or to maintain currency. Practice, yes, because while it's technically correct to say "the plane lands itself," the operation is vastly more elaborate than simply pressing a button marked LAND. For a flight to take advantage of this technology for actual, lowest-visibility conditions, the airplane, crew, and the runway itself all must be equipped and qualified. Fog-prone airports, as you might expect, tend to be outfitted for them.

A newspaper told the story of a flight forced to divert because the pilot wasn't qualified to land in fog. The passengers panicked when the pilot announced that he hadn't been adequately trained. How could this be?

And several years ago, a plane taxiing in foggy weather returned to the gate and the flight attendant announced, "We're sorry, the pilot does not have enough experience to take off." Both of these cases (the former was reported in the UK tabloid, the *Sun*) involve complicated situations that were dumbed into preposterous sounding scenarios.

When visibility drops below certain values, usually less than a quarter-mile, or 1600 feet on the RVR scale, pilots have to perform so-called Category II or Category III ILS approaches, either by hand or in conjunction with autopilot/autoland as described. Because such conditions happen rarely, not all planes are equipped for them, and not all pilots are qualified to fly them. In the British case, conditions called for a Category III, the procedure with the tightest restrictions. Several flights, not just this one, would have been diverted.

For departures it works similarly. When takeoff visibility drops to certain levels, the runway, the airplane, and the pilots all must meet various requirements. In my example the hapless flight attendant was technically correct that her pilot lacked the needed "experience" but was disingenuous, if entertaining, to summarize in such simple language.

One often hears of an airport "closing" during inclement weather. Airports do not close, as such, unless extreme weather renders them totally unusable. More specifically, visibility will drop below what the runways—or an individual crew—are certified to handle. If you've got Category III weather but lack Category III certification, your airport has "closed."

Landing in Boston, we were assigned a last-minute runway change due to boat traffic in the harbor. Had we struck the mast of a ship causing damage to an engine or the landing gear, would the impact be survivable?

Landing gear and engines are great sources of passenger worry, but to an extent they're an airframe's most expendable zones. If I could choose a spot for impact in a scenario like the one described, I'd pick exactly one of these appendages. Damage to a wing is more prone to be fatal. Loss of an engine, as already reviewed, is by rule survivable, while the gear, even if completely torn away, isn't aerodynamically crucial. There have been a few gearless landings—failure to deploy or struts collapsing—none catastrophic and most injury-free. The need to circle while pilots troubleshoot a gear problem, as happens every so often, is no reason to go scribbling your will and testament on the back of a barf bag.

The ships-in-the-harbor runway swap, a semi-regular occurrence at assorted shoreline airports, isn't quite how it sounds. Tracking an ILS, the signals allow for a margin of error, and a ship's mast or smokestack might scratch this buffer zone. Assuming a normal glidepath you'd need a twenty-story mast or smokestack (about 200 feet) to reach a plane's belly a half-mile from the threshold.

On a recent flight we made a terrible landing. We touched down crooked, and thumped onto the pavement with a bang. Why do some pilots land more smoothly than others?

That "terrible landing" was probably a decently executed crosswind touchdown or the effect of some low-level gusts or turbulence. A crosswind landing is rote—a little extra input on the controls to allow for the skewed, "sideways" alignment that is, believe it or not, the properly coordinated technique. Passengers, especially nervous ones, put some weighty stock in the moment of arrival, but a firm touchdown is not necessarily a bad one, and the smoothness of a landing is hardly an accurate benchmark of a pilot's skill *(see pilot skill, page 136)*.

When a plane lands, it sounds like the engines rev up immediately after touchdown. I can't imagine how, but are they reversing?

On most jets the engines indeed reverse, and that is why you hear the surge of power after meeting the pavement. Thrust is redirected by the deployment of deflectors. It's not a true 180-degree redirection, but more of an acutely angled, semiforward vector like the effect of blowing into your cupped hand. If you're seated with a view of the engines, you can see this quite clearly. Once the deflectors are positioned, which takes a second or two, engine power is increased (though only so far; full reverse thrust is only a fraction of available forward thrust). The amount of power needed depends on runway length, weather, and, to an extent, which taxiway turnoff the pilots intend to use. Turboprop engines reverse as well. Propeller blades are able to change angle, forcing air forward rather than backward. (The blades twist longitudinally; the direction of the propeller itself does not change.)

Although reversing is helpful, it's the brakes that do most of the stopping, helped by drag from the flaps and the deployment of spoilers. All those stringent runway restrictions we talked about are calculated *without* use of reverse. Whatever help it gives you is an unmeasured bonus. If your plane's reversers are malfunctioning or inoperable, you still have the numbers. Spoilers, if you've forgotten, are multi-purpose panels that rise above the wing, in this case killing lift and effectively pressing the airplane onto its landing gear, whereby the brakes can take on the work.

I'm tempted to add a blanket statement claiming that no airplane will reverse its engines in flight. For the record, yes, an aircraft *can* reverse in flight. Just as your Honda *can* drive backwards down the interstate at rush hour. Modern planes have apparatus to prohibit inadvertent reversal when not on the ground. In 1991 a 767 operated by Lauda Air, an Austrian charter company, suffered an uncommanded reversal after takeoff from Bangkok. The airplane crashed into the Thai jungle, killing more than 200 people. Boeing redesigned the system.

Where do weather delays come from, and why does the system seem to collapse when the climate goes bad? Planes are stuck in holding patterns or will wait for ninety minutes on a taxiway.

In the majority of cases "weather delay" is a misnomer. More correctly, it's a *traffic* delay—the product of saturation at departure point, destination, or someplace in between. When storms erupt or a fog bank rolls over an airport, separation requirements change. Routings become blocked; flights must be funneled into instrument approach patterns; the dominoes start falling.

When arrival sectors become sufficiently clogged, holding patterns are assigned. Jets will be stacked above and below one another, a thousand feet apart, waiting their turn to land in what becomes a giant, downwardly spiraling helix. To avoid airborne gridlock, departing flights are sometimes kept on the ground until specified, preplanned release times. Things change quickly, for better or worse. Storms pass and airways reopen; storms worsen and they constrict. Visibility improves and airport volume increases; visibility worsens and it's reduced.

Departure slots can be amended on short notice, and this is why the airlines hate when customers go wandering off during gate delays. Once in a while planes are pushed from the gate only to end up languishing for an hour or more on a taxiway or in a holding bay. Nobody enjoys this, and the fault rests with air traffic control's technological shortcomings as well as the vagaries of climate. A flight is sent out; slots are revised before it has a chance to take off, so it sits. If it returns to the gate, there's risk of the whole thing starting over. It's a faster process, though not a more comfortable one, to kill time in the penalty box instead of at the terminal.

It was announced that our flight from Atlanta to La Guardia was canceled because of "thunderstorms over New York." But weather reports and verification with family there revealed no such thing. Was this a lie?

During lousy weather, delays and cancellations snowball and chain react. As they do, complicated information, much of it in constant flux, is transferred from one department to another— from air traffic controller to dispatcher to crewmember to the gate. Each of these departments owns its own procedures and argot, and there's much to be lost in the translation. Believe it or not, the announcement you heard could have meant a number of things, and did not necessarily mean actual rumbles and lightning over La Guardia. The exact location might have been anywhere along the inbound routings. This was minced into "thunderstorms over New York." When the gate agent at last gives you the bad news over the gateside microphone, it's not much different from that game you played in grade school, where a whispered sentence is passed along desk-to-desk and completely transfigured before it reaches the end. I'm not justifying the conveyance of stupid-sounding inaccuracies, but what you hear are muddles, not devious fabrications.

Those catching flights to Boston deal with a similar circumstance all the time. It goes like this: Departure is delayed due to "weather problems" at Logan airport. Just before the new departure time, another announcement is made and the delay is extended. Annoyed passengers rush to telephones. Finally the flight takes off, but not before a forty-minute hop has become a three-hour hassle. Upon landing, passengers are startled to discover clear skies in every direction. The problem is wind. When the wind at Logan happens to blow from the northwest at a strong enough velocity, Logan can use only one of its five runways. The resulting backups are legendary, and this is the "weather problem" that so mystifies Boston-bound travelers.

When a flight is impacted by weather or mechanical problems, who makes the decisions to delay or cancel?

Teams of trained dispatchers, who hold FAA Dispatcher licenses, work in a huge room, typically at the airline's home base or largest hub, that looks like NASA control, handling the nitty-gritty of weather and maintenance. Via radio, phone, or computer, they are in constant contact with all relevant personnel, from on-site mechanics to the crew, even (especially) while aloft, with whom they confer and coordinate.

The interplay between dispatch, crew, mechanics, and customer service is where things often become messy. An airline is often handling the logistics of hundreds of flights at any one time. If staff seem unwilling to dispense information, it's usually just a case of not yet knowing the details, or fear that a situation's complexities will confuse people more than placate them.

Somehow the idea of a "control tower" seems anachronistic. To whom are pilots talking to, and how do flights communicate en route?

Air traffic control, or ATC, is much more than the control tower—that concrete structure with its spinning radar and cluster of antennae, inside which you picture men standing in a windowed room saying things like, "cleared for takeoff." Towers are responsible only for ground movements and airborne traffic within the immediate area.

Let's follow a flight from start to finish across the United States. As we do, keep in mind that airplanes use an electronic unit known as a transponder (two or more are present), to describe whereabouts, speed, and altitude to an ATC radar screen. At some airports, the transponder-radar link can be used to follow planes along foggy taxiways, and though it happens infrequently, a flight can operate gate-to-gate without a single controller ever once laying eyes on the airplane.

Departing from New York, bound for San Francisco, our flight obtains local weather info and flight plan clearances via cockpit datalink computer. When ready to taxi, the crew radios for pushback clearance, followed by another call for taxi instructions. Getting from gate to runway can involve a half dozen conversations with the likes of "clearance delivery," "gate control," "ground control," and others. These entities may or may not be physically located in the control tower, but are always somewhere at the airport. Finally a flight will be cleared for takeoff by the tower.

Only moments after liftoff we are handed over to "departure control," which follows us on radar, issuing turns, altitudes, and so forth as the plane is sequenced into the overlying route structure. During a single interaction with departure control, a flight can progress through several subsectors, each maintained by a separate controller.

Once at higher altitude we're guided by a series of Air Route Traffic Control Centers (ARTCC), commonly called "Center"— Boston Center, New York Center, etc. They maintain huge swaths of sky, rendering them somewhat irrelevant to their namesake identifiers. Often, Center facilities are located in secure buildings far from an airport. Boston Center, for instance, in charge of airspace extending from southern New England to the Canadian Maritimes, resides in a building in Nashua, New Hampshire. Centers too are broken down into subsectors, each in the hands of individual controllers. Crossing the country, we make ten or more radio frequency changes, in touch with a new person each time.

Eventually, descending into San Francisco, the above happens more or less in reverse. Center first hands us to "approach control," and if the weather is bad and arrivals are backing up, these are the folks who'll assign a holding pattern. Around the time you hear the landing gear plunking into position the crew is given over to the tower for landing clearance, and then it's another conversational gambol with ground and gate before docking safely and, of course, on time.

Terminology changes when we leave the USA, but basic concepts are the same everywhere. Over the maw of open ocean, devoid of radar and real-time air traffic control, planes are monitored remotely and spaced apart using datalink or long-range radio. English, I might add, is the official language of civil flight and is spoken by controllers and pilots worldwide.

Flying to Europe from Florida, our routing took us up over northeastern Canada and close to Iceland. Looking on a map this makes no sense.

Thanks to the hard work of imperialist European explorers, and later confirmed by NASA photography, we have determined the earth is round (technically it's not a sphere but a geoid, but we're not going there). Okay, we can live with that. But are we, in our attempts to decorate our offices and educate our kids, giving a false impression of the oceans and continents?

When the earth is crushed from its natural (round) state into a strictly horizontal one, it becomes distorted as the divisions of latitude and longitude stretch apart. Depending on the layout used—what cartographers call "projection"—the distortion can be grotesque. Many of us have grown up believing, for instance, that Greenland is about ten times larger than it really is, thanks to the preposterous polar dimensions of the Mercator projection. Some people call this "the Rand McNally Syndrome." What this all means is that accurately surmising a long-distance, point-to-point course on a globe is very different from measuring one on a flat map.

Try it yourself: Go and fetch three items: a globe, an atlas, and a length of dental floss. (We'll assume your atlas is one of those Americentric maps with the United States in the center.) With your gear in hand, let's travel between New York City and Hong Kong.

First, lay out the shortest distance using only the atlas. The floss will point slightly southwest from New York. It will pass over San Francisco, across the center of the Pacific near Midway Island, then south of Japan before reaching China. A very long distance. Indeed it is. But now, floss your way to Hong Kong using the globe. Almost at once you will realize how lavishly impractical the first route is. It's much less circuitous simply to bend your string *over the top* of the planet. And if you're taking one of Continental Airlines' 777s on this very flight, don't be baffled when you see the frozen Hudson Bay and Siberian tundra passing beneath you rather than the Golden Gate Bridge and warm Pacific seas. The shortest distance between New York and Hong Kong is not southwesterly; it's north.

That's the extreme, but the principle applies to many long-range pairings. Between continents, airplanes do not fly the straight lines evident on your atlas or wall map. They follow what are called "great circle" routes, the leanest mileage totals along a sphere, accounting for curvature and which we've mimicked with the floss test.

As things tend to go, real life operations aren't so cleanly theoretical. Flights over the North Atlantic (and parts of the Pacific too) adhere to predetermined paths called "tracks," for example, while political frictions between countries mandate various overland zigzags. But these are still in keeping, overall, with great circle courses. And this is why passengers between America and Europe discover themselves not just high up, but high *up*, over Nova Scotia, Newfoundland, and occasionally into the icy realm of "sixty north," the latitude almost scraping the tip of Greenland. Bound for Europe, even from Miami, that'll be Boston, Halifax, and Gander down below.

One night at Kennedy airport I gave what I thought were accurate instructions to a group of Muslims crouched on the floor of Terminal One looking for Mecca. It seemed to me they were facing more toward Connecticut, and I suggested they adjust their prayer rugs a few southeastward degrees. I should have known better, because the most efficient routing between New York and Mecca is not southeast, as it would appear on a map, but *northeast*.

Required to periodically align themselves with a point thousands of miles away, many Muslims know how this works. To face the holy Kaaba at Mecca, they employ what's called the *qibla*, which is the shortest distance to Mecca from where they're standing, or kneeling—a kind of Islamic great circle. (It is said Mohammed could ascertain the *qibla* from anywhere without aid of scientific instruments.) My friends at Kennedy were searching for their *qibla*, only to find quibble instead with an itinerant pilot who was thinking flat when he should've been thinking round.

Passengers aboard Saudi Arabian Airlines, for one, can avoid such disorientation thanks to the airline's satellite-aided "*qibla* compass," providing a constant update of direction and distance to Mecca. Saudi pilots, though, as well as pilgrims on *hajj*, are probably just as interested in the shortest distance to Jeddah, about forty miles west of Mecca. Jeddah is where the airport is.

Which planes have the longest range?

Bear in mind that a plane's size isn't always a good indicator of how far it can fly. The old Airbus A300, probably the best example, was built specifically for short- to medium-haul markets even though it can accommodate 250 people. Certain models of nine-passenger executive jets, on the other hand, can stay aloft for ten hours.

Upon entry into service in 2006, the Boeing 777-200LR will have the longest duration of any jetliner, able to span 9,000 nautical miles without refueling. Pakistan International and Taiwan's Eva Air have placed the earliest orders. Almost every major city-pair on earth will be connectable with this astoundingly long-legged aircraft, including the previously unimaginable New York–Sydney. Until then, winner is the A340-500, first flown by Emirates and presently doing eighteen hour marathons for Singapore Airlines *(see longest flights, page 261)*. Current variants of the 777 and 747 have comparable but slightly lesser capabilities.

Notice I say variants. Watch the dashes. There's not just an A340, there's the A340-200, −300, −500, and −600. At Boeing you'll discover 200s, −300s, −500s, −LRs, −ERs (for Long Range and Extended Range), and so forth. Technical options—engine types, auxiliary fuel tanks—affect endurance, and it's not always fair to say, out of hand, that one plane has greater reach than another. Does an A340 outdistance a 747? Some do, some don't. And a larger suffix might not tell the story. An A340-500 has longer range than the A340-600. A 767-200ER outlasts a 767-300ER. If you enjoy graphs and charts abounding with asterisks and fine print, go to the manufacturer's websites and knock yourself out. What it comes down to is this: The Boeing 747, 777, and Airbus A340 are the longest rangers. When it flies, the A380 will join them.

Whenever I fly from California to New England, the pilot never fails to mention we'll be passing over Gardner, Massachusetts. Gardner is a tiny town in the middle of nowhere. Why is a spot like this so relevant to a plane at 35,000 feet?

Little Gardner, Massachusetts, is home to a radio beacon used as a sequence point for air traffic, prevalently noted on certain maps and charts.

Despite advances in direct-route, satellite-based GPS, point-to-point routings using ground stations, known as VORs (Very-high-frequency Omnidirectional Range), remain the norm in the United States. Whether flying cross-country or up and down the coasts, planes travel between these facilities in a connect-the-dots pattern. If this sounds anachronistic, it is. Even if equipped with GPS equipment, a plane is still subjugated by air traffic control's fundamentally outmoded standard. Crews may use GPS to determine a VOR's position, creating virtual waypoints in lieu of homing to the actual beacon, but conceptually it's still a ground-based network. In late 2003 the FAA revealed its "road map," spelling out a twenty-year transition to satellite-based traffic management. That's about fifteen years too conservative, and hence we look forward to another two decades of congested airways.

Elsewhere around the world things aren't much improved. In

the highly competitive market between Europe and Southeast Asia, flights are hobbled by political frictions as well as outmoded air traffic control infrastructures. Long-haul veterans like Lufthansa and Qantas, with much at stake, have worked with IATA (International Air Transport Association—a trade organization comprised of hundreds of airlines) and local authorities to ease overflight restrictions and circuitous patterns above China, India, and the Middle East.

Across oceans aircraft follow more straightforward paths. It's a similar connect-the-dots routine, only now the dots are invisible meetings of latitude and longitude. Planes follow long strings of lat-long fixes (possibly a curved string, conforming to those great circles). If GPS isn't on hand for this, something called INS (Inertial Navigation System) remains fairly common. Entirely self-contained, INS hardware uses complex, in-unit gyroscopes to calculate location. Passenger jets certified for oceanic crossings are outfitted with three independent INS boxes.

If you've ever paid attention to the air-ground communications through a plane's entertainment system, you've probably been mystified by the calls of controllers directing flights toward all kinds of strange, fantastical-sounding places. "United 626, proceed to ZAPPY," you'll hear. Or, "Southwest 1407, cleared to WOPPO." A look at a navigational chart reveals that the entire United States, and the rest of the world for that matter, is overlaid by thousands of point-in-space fixes, or "intersections," that carry these peculiar five-letter monikers. I invented ZAPPY and WOPPO myself, but I'll bet they're out there somewhere. They are determined by angles and distances from VORs, or else by crisscrosses of latitude and longitude, allowing them to exist virtually anywhere, even over the middle of an ocean.

Once in a while intersections are coined in folksy reference to geographic or cultural characteristics below. SCROD is a transatlantic gateway fix off the coast of Labrador. BOSOX is one not far from where I live (baseball fans will understand). God only knows what's going on beneath BLOWN, LAYED, and BAABY, a trio of intersections over West Virginia and Pennsylvania.

Which are the busiest airports?

Most of the busiest airports are hubs, meaning large numbers of travelers—sometimes the majority—are temporary visitors in transit between flights. Atlanta's Hartsfield International sees more footsteps than any other airport on the planet, but the bulk of them are confined to the concourse. The hub concept thus allows small population centers to be represented by large airports. At Charlotte, North Carolina, Douglas International is the thirty-fourth busiest in the world, owing its out-of-scale aerocommerce to US Airways. Cincinnati and Salt Lake City are comparable examples, courtesy of Delta. You can fly to London, Paris, and Frankfurt nonstop from Cincinnati, a place most Brits, French, and Germans probably couldn't locate on a map.

By pure passenger volume for the year, as researched by *Air Transport World* and the Airports Council International, here are the ten largest for 2002. Note the position of Denver, which would have no business here at all if it weren't for United's in-transit feed. O'Hare is a rarity in that *two* major airlines, United and American, both run megahubs from the premises. Connecting passengers are counted only once:

1. ATL Atlanta, USA (76.9 million)
2. ORD Chicago-O'Hare, USA (66.5 million)
3. LHR London-Heathrow, UK (63.3 million)
4. HND Tokyo-Haneda, Japan (61.1 million)
5. LAX Los Angeles, USA (56.2 million)
6. DFW Dallas/Ft. Worth, USA (52.8 million)
7. FRA Frankfurt, Germany (48.5 million)
8. CDG Paris-Charles de Gaulle (48.3 million)
9. AMS Amsterdam, Netherlands (40.7 million)
10. DEN Denver, USA (35.7 million)

Plenty of cities are equipped with more than one airport. London has five, and New York's cluster threesome—Kennedy, Newark, and the comparatively smaller La Guardia—are each among the world's forty busiest. By combining passenger totals at multiairport cities, we can invent a new category, that of the busiest metro areas:

1. London-Heathrow, Gatwick, Stansted, London City, and Luton (117.9 million)
2. Tokyo-Haneda and Narita (90 million)

3. Chicago-O'Hare, Midway, and Gary (83.8 million)
4. New York-JFK, Newark, La Guardia, Islip, White Plains, and Newburg (81.1 million)
5. Atlanta (76.9 million)

Notice Atlanta, even with no second fiddle, is strong enough to hold the top five. If you've never heard of Tokyo's Haneda, it's a large in-city property serving only the domestic market. Think of it as a Japanese La Guardia. We shouldn't go too far with this, as it gets into the definition of what, exactly, constitutes a metro area. Islip's MacArthur airport is fifty miles from Manhattan.

Measured by takeoffs and landings, also known as "movements," it all changes. The catch here is that smaller craft count no different from a 747. In Boston, for example, close to half of all movements are regionals, lofting it to twenty-fifth place for movements versus thirty-seventh in number of people. Here's your score:

1. ORD Chicago-O'Hare, USA (924,000)
2. ATL Atlanta, USA (890,000)
3. DFW Dallas/Ft. Worth (765,000)
4. LAX Los Angeles, USA (645,000)
5. PHX Phoenix, USA (546,000)
6. CDG Paris-Charles de Gaulle (510,000)
7. MSP Minneapolis/St. Paul, USA (507,000)
8. LAS Las Vegas, USA (497,000)
9. DEN Denver, USA (494,000)
10. DTW Detroit, USA (491,000)

This allows a beautiful segue into safety. From above we realize that in 2002 at the top two airports alone, Chicago O'Hare and Atlanta, almost two million airplanes arrived or departed, transporting 143 million people in the process. Not a single one crashed and not a single life was lost.

I'm intrigued by the three-letter codes for airports. Many make no sense.

The three-letter abbreviations are devised by IATA. There also are four-letter versions from ICAO, the civil aviation branch of the United Nations, but these are used only for navigation and technical purposes.

If not blatantly obvious, like BOS for Boston or BRU for Brussels, most are fairly intuitive, such as LHR at London Heathrow or KIX for Osaka's Kansai International. Many of the outwardly arbitrary ones are carryovers from former names for the airport. MCO is derived from McCoy Field, the original name for Orlando International. Chicago O'Hare's identifier, ORD, pays honors to the old Orchard Field.

Others are geographical associations or personal tributes, some more obscure than others. In Rio de Janeiro your plane will land at Galeão, on Governor's Island (Ilha do Governador), lending to the code GIG. On Maui, OGG is homage to Bertram Hogg, Hawaii native and pioneer of Pacific flying.

In one of those moments of American puritanical excess, a campaign was launched in 2002 to change the identifier for Sioux

City, Iowa, from SUX to something less objectionable. The code, and some pleasantly roguish charm along with it, was retained. The Finns don't mind HEL as their capital city, and neither do the Syrians have a problem with DAM. Not being intimate with Japanese vulgarity, I'm unsure what that country's opinion is to FUK, the code for Fukuoka. Traveling FUK-DAM-HEL, try not to speak in acronyms when the agent asks where you're going.

4

Are You Experienced? The Awe and Oddity of Piloting

. . .

The Exploding Toilet and Other Embarrassments
NOT ALL MISTAKES ARE FATAL. SOME ARE WORSE.

An old bromidic adage defines the business of flying planes as long stretches of boredom punctuated by moments of sheer terror. Moments of sheer ridiculousness, maybe, are equally as harrowing. One young pilot, when he was twenty-two and trying to impress the pretty Christine Collingworth with a sightseeing circuit in a friend's Cessna, highlighted the seduction by whacking his forehead into the jutting metal pitot tube hanging from the wing. Earning a famous "Cessna dimple," so he chose to think, would be the stupidest thing he'd ever do in or around an airplane.

That was a long time ago, and a long way from this same pilot's mind during a late-night cargo flight. It's eleven p.m. and the airplane, an old DC-8 freighter loaded with pineapples, is somewhere over the Bermuda Triangle, bound from San Juan, Puerto Rico, to Cincinnati. The night is dark and quiet, void of moonlight, conversation, and for that matter worry. The crew of three is tired, and this will be their last leg in a week's rotation that has sent them from New York to Belgium and back again, onward to Mexico, and now to the Caribbean.

They are mesmerized by the calming drone of high-bypass turbofans and the deceptively peaceful noise of five-hundred knots of frigid wind cleaved along the cockpit windows. Such a setting, when you really think about it, ought to be enough to scare the living shit from any sensible person. We have no business, maybe, being up there, participants in such an inherently dangerous balance between naïve solitude and instant death, distracted by paperwork and chicken sandwiches while screaming along, higher than Mount Everest and at the speed of sound in a forty-year-old assemblage of machinery. But such philosophizing is for poets, not pilots, and also makes for exceptionally bad karma. No mystical ruminations were in the job description for these three airmen, consummate professionals who long ago sold their souls to the more practical-minded muses of technology and luck.

Our pilot, whose name is Patrick Smith, born Patrick R. Santo-suosso of Revere, Massachusetts, a fourth-generation descendant of Neapolitan olive growers, is one of these consummate professionals. Now 34, he has seen his career stray oddly from its intended course, his ambitions of flying gleaming new passenger jets to distant ports-of-call have given way to the coarser world of air cargo, to sleepless, back-of-the-clock timetables, the greasy glare of warehouse lights, and the roar of forklifts—realities that have aroused a low note of disappointment that rings constantly in the back of his brain. He is the second officer. His station, a sideways-turned chair and a great, blackboard-sized panel of instruments, is set against the starboard wall.

He stands up from the second officer's seat and walks out of the cockpit, closing the door behind him. Here he enters the plane's only other accessible zone during flight, the small entryway vestibule adjacent to the main cabin door. It contains a life raft, oven, cooler, some storage space, and the lavatory. His plan is simple enough—to get himself a Diet Coke. The soft drinks are in a cardboard box on the floor, in a six-pack strapped together with one of those clear plastic harnesses so threatening to sea turtles and small children. These plastic rings are banned at home, but apparently perfectly legal in the Caribbean, where there are, of course, lots of sea turtles and small children. The pilot is thinking about this as he reaches for a can, weighing the injustices of the world, philosophizing, daydreaming, ruminating—things that, again, his manuals neither command nor endorse, for perhaps good reason.

He unstraps a Coke and decides to put the remaining ones in the cooler to chill. The cooler, a red, lift-top Coleman that you'd buy at Sears, sits in front of the lavatory and is packed with bags of ice. The pilot drops in the cans, but now the cooler will not close. There's too much ice. One of the bags will have to go. So he pulls one out and shuts the lid. Decisions, decisions. Which checklist do I initiate? Which valve do I command closed? Which circuit breakers do I pull? How do I keep us alive and this contraption intact? And what to do, now, with an extra sopping-wet bag of ice? Well, the pilot will do what he *always* does with an extra bag of ice. He will open the bag and dump it down the toilet. This he has done so often that the sound of a hundred cubes hitting the metal bowl is a familiar one.

This time, though, for reasons he hasn't realized yet, there are no cubes; or, more correctly, there is one huge cube. He rips open the bag, which is greenish and slightly opaque, and out slides a long, single block of ice, probably two pounds' worth, which clatters off the rim and splashes into the bowl. There it is met, of course, by the caustic blue liquid one always finds in airplane toilets—the strange chemical cocktail that so efficiently and brightly neutralizes our organic contributions. The fluid washes over the ice. He hits the flush and it's drawn into the hole and out of sight. He turns, clutching the empty bag and worrying still about the dangers of plastic rings and turtles, picturing some poor endangered hawksbill choking to death. It's just not fair.

And it's now that the noise begins. As he steps away, the pilot hears a deep and powerful burble, which immediately repeats itself and seems to emanate from somewhere in the bowels of the plane. How to describe it? It's similar to the sound your own innards might make if you've eaten an entire pizza, or perhaps swallowed Drano, amplified many times over. The pilot stops and a quick shot of adrenaline pulses into his veins. What was *that*? It grows louder. Then there's a rumble, a vibration passes up through his feet, and from behind him comes a loud swishing noise.

He turns and looks at the toilet. But it has, for all practical purposes, disappeared, and where it once rested he now finds what he will later describe only as: *a vision*. In place of the commode roars a fluorescent blue waterfall, a huge, heaving cascade of toilet fluid thrust waist-high into the air and splashing into all four corners of the lavatory. Pouring from the top of this volcano, like smoke out of a factory chimney, is a rapidly spreading pall of what looks like steam. He closes his eyes tightly for a second, then reopens them. He does this not for the benefit of unwitnessed theatrics, or even to create an embellishment for later use in a story. He does so because, for the first time in his life, he truly *does not believe* what is cast in front of him.

The fountain grows taller, and he sees that the toilet is not actually spraying, but *bubbling*—a geyser of lathering blue foam topped with a thick white fog. And suddenly he realizes what's happened. It was not a block of ice, exactly, that he fed to the toilet. It was a block of *dry* ice.

To combine dry ice with liquid is to initiate the turbulent, and rather unstoppable, chemical reaction now under way before our unfortunate friend. The effect, though in our case on a much grander scale, is similar to the mixing of baking soda with vinegar, or dumping water into a Friolator, an exciting experiment those of you who've worked in restaurants have probably experienced: The boiling oil will have nothing to do with the water, discharging its elements in a violent surge of bubbles. Normally when the caterers use dry ice, it's packed apart in smaller, square-shaped bags you can't miss. Today, though, an extra-large allotment was stuffed into a regular old ice cube bag—two pounds of solid carbon dioxide mixing quite unhappily with a tankful of acid.

Within seconds a wide blue river begins to flow out of the lav and across the floor, where a series of tracks, panels, and gullies promptly splits it into several smaller rivers, each leading away to a different nether region beneath the main deck of the DC-8. The liquid moves rapidly along these paths, spilling off into the crevices. It's your worst bathroom nightmare at home or in a hotel—clogging up the shitter at midnight and watching it overflow. Except this time it's a Technicolor eruption of flesh-eating poison, dribbling into the seams of an airplane down into the entrails to freeze itself around cables or short out bundles of vital wiring. Our pilot once read a report about a toilet reservoir somehow becoming frozen in the back of a 727. A chunk of blue ice was ejected overboard and sucked into an engine, causing the entire thing, pylon and all, to tear away and drop to earth.

And the pilot knows his cataract is not going to stop until either the carbon dioxide is entirely evaporated or the tank of blue death is entirely drained. Meanwhile, the white steam, the evaporating carbon dioxide, is filling the cabin with vapor like the smoke show at a rock concert. He decides to get the captain.

Our captain tonight, as fate would have it, is a boisterous and slightly crazy Scandinavian. Let's call him Jens. Jens is a tall, square-jawed Norwegian with graying, closely cropped curls and an animated air of imperious cocksure. Jens is one of those guys who makes everybody laugh simply by walking into a room, though whether or not he's trying to is never clear. He is sitting in the captain's chair. The sun has set hours ago but he is still wearing Ray-Bans.

"Jens, come here fast! I need your help."

Jens nods to the first officer and unbuckles his belt. This is an airline captain, a confident four-striper trained and ready for any variety of airborne calamity—engine failures, fires, bombs, windshear. What will he find back there? Jens steps into the entryway and is greeted not by any of a thousand different training scenarios, but by a psychedelic fantasy of color and smoke, a wall of white fog, and the fuming blue witch's cauldron, the outfall from which now covers the entire floor, from the entrance of the cockpit to the enormous nylon safety net that separates the crew from its load of pineapples.

Jens stares. Then he turns to his young second officer and puts a hand on his shoulder, a gesture of both fatherly comfort and surrendering camaraderie, as if to say, "Don't worry, son, I'll clean all this up," or maybe, "Down with the ship we go." He sighs, nods toward the fizzing, disgorging bowl, and says, with a tone of surprisingly *un*ironic pride: "She's got quite a head on her, doesn't she?"

But what can they do? And in one of those dreaded realizations pilots are advised to avoid, that insulation between cockpit calm and atmospheric anarchy looks thin indeed. An extrapolated vision of horror: the riveted aluminum planks bending apart, the wind rushing in, explosive depressurization, death, the first airliner—no, the first *vehicle*—in history to crash because of an overflowing toilet. Into the sea, where divers and salvage ships will haul up the wreckage, detritus trailing from mauled, unrecognizable pieces while investigators shake their heads. At least, the pilot thinks, odds are nobody will ever know the truth, the cold ocean carrying away the evidence. He's good as dead, but saved, maybe, from immortal embarrassment. A dash of mystique awaits him, the same that met Saint-Exupéry at the bottom of the Mediterranean, another lousy pilot who got philosophical and paid the price. Maybe *he* blew up the toilet too: *Probable cause—unknown*.

"Call flight control," commands Jens, hoping a dose of authority will interject some clarity into a scene that is obviously and hopelessly absurd. "Get a patch with maintenance and explain what happened."

The pilot rushes back to the cockpit to call the company's maintenance staff. He fires up the high-frequency radios, small black boxes that can bounce the human voice, and any of its associated embarrassments, up off the ionosphere and halfway around the world if need be. He will announce his predicament to the mechanics, and also to any of dozens of other crews monitoring the same frequency. Even before keying the mike he can see the looks and hear the wisecracks from the Delta and United pilots in their state-of-the-art 777s, Mozart soothing their passengers through Bose headsets, flight attendants wiping down the basins while somewhere in the night sky three poor souls in a Cold War relic are trapped in a blue scatological hell, struggling helplessly with a flood of shit and chemicals.

"You say the *toilet exploded*?" Maintenance is on the line, incredulous but not particularly helpful. "Well, um, not sure. Should be okay. Nothing below the cabin there to worry about. Press on, I guess." Thanks. Click.

Jens has now grabbed the extension wand for the fire extinguisher—a hollow metal pole the length of a harpoon—and is shoving it down into the bowl trying to agitate the mixture to a stop. Several minutes have passed, and a good ten gallons have streamed their way onto the floor and beyond. Up front, the first officer has no idea what's going on. Looking behind him, his view mostly blocked by the circuit breaker panels and cockpit door, this is what he sees: a haze of white odorless smoke, and his captain yelping with laughter and thrusting at something with a long metal pole.

The pilot stands aside, watching Jens do battle. This was the same little kid who dreamed of becoming a 747 captain, the embodiment of all that was, and could still be, glamorous and exciting about aviation. And poor Jens, whose ancestors ploughed this same Atlantic in longboats, ravenous for adventure and conquest, a twenty-first-century Viking jousting with a broken toilet.

So it goes, and by the time the airplane touches down, its plumbing finally at rest, each and every employee at the cargo hub, clued in by the amused mechanics who received our distress call, already knows the story of the idiot who poured dry ice into the crapper. His socks and hundred-dollar Rockports have been badly damaged, while the walls, panels, and placards aboard aircraft 806 are forever dyed a heavenly azure.

The crew bus pulls up to the stairs, and as the pilots step on board the driver looks up and says excitedly, "Which one of you did it?"

According to several accounts, pilots are notoriously cheap. Is this not ironic considering how much money they make?

If pilots are cheap it's because it sometimes takes them years and years of slugging it out at low-paying regional airlines before they ever make a halfway decent salary. The pilots on the upper parts of a major airline's seniority list indeed make a good living, but it may not have come easy. Flying, it has been said, is much like acting, painting, or playing minor league ball (or trying your luck at a book). Rewards loom for the fortunate, but many toil in extended, even perpetual purgatory for their art.

For a civilian pilot with a fresh commercial license and a few hundred logbook hours, entry-level jobs are not only tough to come by, but financially humiliating. If a pilot is lucky he'll slip straight from flight school, where his FAA qualifications ran $25,000 or more, to a first officer position at a regional airline, where starting salaries are $20,000 or less. Even that is best case. More likely he'll first spend some time flight instructing, towing banners, or engaging in any manner of ad hoc experience building—the pilot equivalent of odd jobs.

Once established at a regional he can look forward to at least a couple, and more likely several, years of hard work before a major will take his resume seriously. And he'll still need the hiring trends—i.e. the economy and industry health—to hold favorably, as well as a good dose of luck. Then, at a typical large airline, a first-year pilot will earn about $30,000. No, there are no missing digits there. It rises sharply thereafter, but probably not as sharply as you think.

If you find that difficult to believe, obviously you've been paying too close attention to the many politicians, commentators, and op-ed columnists who've taken to shaming those spoiled airline pilots for "making $300,000 a year and working fifty hours a month."

The number of pilots receiving such salaries—almost always gray-haired captains nearing the mandatory retirement age of sixty—are a small fraction of an airline's total roster, which in the case of giants like United and American is a list of almost ten thousand names. These are fellows the airlines, and sometimes politicians, make examples of during contract negotiations, but in truth they make up only a portion, albeit a high-profile one, of all pilots out there. During the Comair strike in 2001, union activists scored a PR victory by pointing out that a first-year pilot with a family qualified for food stamps.

As for the lazy schedule, a pilot works fifty hours a month the way a football player works an hour each week. Not counted in that total are long stretches of time between flights, off-duty deadheading, paperwork, and uncountable nights in hotel rooms. These ancillaries constitute "work" by anybody's definition, but are *not* counted in the block-hour examples put forth.

The trick is to grab a seniority number as quickly as possible—and to hope for the best. Rewards come later, not sooner. And on the way be prepared for a multiyear layoff or two and the industry's cyclical scourges. Risks are inherent in many professions, but earning all the needed licenses and ratings, at least as a civilian, is extremely expensive, and you will not be recouping your outlay anytime soon. And you can forgo any plans for a predictable career.

When it's all said and done, the business of flying planes is a blue-collar job, much as some pilots are loath to admit. We are sometimes so defensive about what it means, or doesn't mean, to be a professional, that we're unable to accept this, especially as the industry in whole loses more and more of the public's respect. Regardless of collar color, we're in no way off the hook as far as needing to maintain the highest standards; and a berth at an established carrier, at least when the ink is running black and people aren't crashing planes into buildings, is a good one.

Nevertheless, many people put the onus of the industry's difficulties on labor unions, particularly those representing pilots. Is there some merit to this?

To the extent that wages and benefits comprise an airline's largest expenditure, yes. In the United States, between 29 and 42 percent of the largest airlines' cost pies are cut for labor. But scapegoating unions as the malevolent root of the industry's woes is a tough sell. And what could be more insulting than executives awarding themselves millions in protective perks, as happened in 2003 after the worst-ever losses in airline history? Such ill-timed gestures led to the resignation of American Airlines CEO Donald Carty.

After the 2001 terrorist attacks, the U.S. government eventually offered some $20 billion in direct aid, loan guarantees, tax relief, and security reimbursements to the battered industry. But only if sweeping reductions in labor costs were negotiated first. Whether such demands represent true economic desperation as opposed to punitive politics depends who you ask. Says Duane Woerth, head of ALPA (the Air Line Pilots Association—the world's largest pilot union) "a war is being waged on organized labor."

By 2003 American saved $2 billion per year in a labor package that put 2,500 of its pilots on the street. US Airways, first of the ancients to declare bankruptcy after September 11 (and first to emerge), won extensive givebacks, including termination of its pilots' pension plan. United got $2.56 billion in annual concessions from unions, 44 percent of it from pilots, who agreed to a 30 percent reduction in pay. A 30 percent cut might not be devastating to senior pilots earning $200,000, but it certainly influences the lives of thousands of others who bring home a fraction of that amount, provided they still have jobs at all.

When concessions are the topic, pilots are an easy target and tend to be the focus of attention, as their average salaries are highest among an airline's frontline workforce. But as you probably realize by now, I get defensive when people play fast and loose with the image of pilots as overpaid and unproductive. I hate having to trundle out the same old reminder, but most pilots do *not* bring home the obscenely spectacular paychecks often cited.

As the industry started to flail, senior captains at United were turned into poster children by aghast politicians and media sources. From the Senate floor to the microphones of National Public Radio came examples of six-digit incomes of senior pilots who "work only fifty hours a month." The qualifier is "senior." In these apocryphals of populist outrage, nobody ever mentions the pilots making thirty-five, fifty-five, or seventy thousand. Or, at the regionals, seventeen, twenty-one, or thirty thousand. And when those pay reductions are hashed out, do you think the lower rungs are exempt? Many are handed furlough notices. There's also a degree of distortion in what can seem, on the face of it, a grossly extravagant W-2. After years of struggling, with perhaps a couple of multiyear layoffs thrown in, these late-in-life payoffs aren't necessarily as vulgar as they appear.

Do I think a senior captain deserves to make $250,000? The short answer is no, but neither does a first officer deserve $25,000. Admittedly this sets up a trap: Does a dentist "deserve" to make $200,000? Or, through the other end of the telescope, does a teacher "deserve" $22,000? The trap is making moral judgments on a market-determined product. For a while, the market supported the $250,000 pilot, so there are $250,000 pilots. If the market no longer supports them, they will go away.

The seniority system, not without its benefits, has deeply solidified a top-heavy concentration of earnings that can render average or median figures meaningless. Industry average salary for a co-pilot is about $70,000. Tell that to a third-year worker at a regional reporting $24,000 to the IRS. By economies of scale, the quarter-million-dollar pilot was made possible thanks to widebody aircraft bringing in revenue from hundreds of passengers. An economist (or a management executive) might contend that a fifty-seat regional jet offers no such possibility. Which is true, and nobody is advocating that an RJ captain be paid the same as his counterpart on a 777. But if we apply some version of temperance to the high-end salary, let's also address the low end.

Spreading out the wealth wouldn't drastically change an airline's overall tab, and is maybe the most equitable solution. This is a gripe, if indeed a given pilot sees it as one, to be taken up between pilots and their unions rather than unions and the airlines. To beat up on the way organized labor might have skewed the system to foster inequities within its own ranks is one thing. Fertilizing the overgrown conception of pilots as avaricious prima donnas is something else.

How are pilots evaluated for raises or promotions?

Within an airline, everything—and I do mean everything—from promotions to route assignments to vacations, happens per seniority. Pilots (and flight attendants too) bid their preferences for position, aircraft type, and schedule, and are awarded according to rank. A first officer becomes captain not when his boss thinks he's earned a shot, but when his number is up.

When business is bad and airlines are contracting, the same thing occurs in reverse: Captains become first officers, and those nearest the bottom become cabdrivers. (As this book is prepared, more than ten thousand airline pilots have been furloughed in the United States.) It's all very structured and, if I can say so without refueling the ire of my brethren, blue collar. The process has little to do with merit and everything to do with timing. Any time a pilot takes up shop at a new airline, he does so at the bottom of the list and is back to making a probationary salary. There is no sideways transfer of skills or pay. If, whether by choice or through the forces of bankruptcy or layoff, a pilot takes a position at another airline, he resets that fancy watch and begins again, effectively as a brand-new rookie. Yes, this is industry standard, and it's one of the reasons pilots are often militant when it comes to labor issues. They are scared shitless of having to start over at the bottom somewhere.

What is the difference between a pilot, copilot, and captain?

All modern aircraft are flown by a two-person crew consisting of a captain and a first officer. The latter is referred to colloquially as the copilot. Both are fully qualified to fly the plane in all regimes of flight, and will do so in alternating turns. If a crew is going from New York to Chicago to Seattle, the captain will fly the first leg and the first officer will fly the second. The latter is not on hand as a helpful apprentice. The captain does not say to his grateful underling, "Here, son, how about you take it for a minute."

The pilot not flying is still plenty busy and has a long list of chores, working the communications radios, programming navigational computers, reading checklists, and so forth. Regardless of who's driving, the captain has ultimate authority over the flight, and a larger paycheck to go with it. Captains wear four stripes on their sleeves and epaulets, first officers three. Outside North America you'll notice slightly different designs with stars, crests, or other markings.

On long hauls, one or more relief pilots are on hand to temporarily take the place of a captain or first officer during designated rest periods. In most cases they're full-fledged pilots dealt such duties through seniority, or lack thereof.

A few older aircraft still in service, such as the 727 or classic model 747, require a third pilot. This is the second officer or "flight engineer," whose workstation, including a large, wall-mounted instrument panel, is on the starboard side of the cockpit behind the first officer. His job is the management of a multitude of onboard systems—electrical, hydraulic, fuel, pressurization, and others—as well as backing up the captain and first officer. If you're wondering about the navigator, that's a job description that hasn't existed on most Western-built planes since the 1960s. Maybe you're remembering the Howard Borden character from the old *Bob Newhart Show*.

How long does training take at an airline? And what qualifications are prerequisite?

A certain pilot took advantage of parental generosity to fund his initial training. He took flying lessons during high school, an hour at a time, and earned a private pilot's license before he turned twenty. From there he added various other ratings and became a flight instructor, eventually accumulating about fifteen hundred hours in various Pipers and Cessnas before getting a job as a first officer with a regional airline in 1990.

A decade later, when he was at last hired by a large airline, he'd amassed about 5,000 logbook hours, most in regional airliners and the rest as a second officer on a cargo jet. That's a fairly typical resume, though applicants from the armed forces have, on average, fewer total hours than civilians. Most airlines ask for a college degree, though it needn't be within a science or technology-related field.

Pilots are not hired for experience per se. During the interview process, which can take one or two days, a candidate with 3,000 hours is not always outqualified by somebody with two, three, or four times that many. Once the prerequisites are met, all candidates are on equal footing and, as in most professions, personality and overall impression become the make-or-break factors. I wouldn't call experience overrated, exactly, but it's something like that.

Once hired, airline curricula are highly alike. Whether to fly a Regional Jet or a 777, the duration and structure of the training regimen are about the same. A group of new-hires will sit through two weeks of company indoctrination and regulations lectures, then move on to aircraft-specific flight training. The latter involves classroom work with instructors, multiple sessions in computerized cockpit mock-ups, and finally a week or two in the big, full-motion simulators. The entire program, start to finish, runs anywhere from a month to ten weeks, influenced mainly by simulator availability. Refresher qualification usually lasts three or four days and is a mandatory yearly, sometimes twice-yearly, event.

Everyone has heard how astoundingly true-to-life the simulators are, and maybe you assume this contains some exaggeration—an element of proud, technophilic bragging. I assure you that isn't the case, and a session of mock disaster in "the box" is something hardly believable until you've done it. *Lived* it, is the better word, since the ride is pretty much a full mental and physical immersion. It would almost be fun, if only a pilot's job weren't in the balance every time.

Are pilots trained to fly more than one airplane at a time? Can the pilot of a 747 also fly a 757?

Yes and no; mostly no. Management and training staff are occasionally cross-qualified, but the rank and file is assigned to specific aircraft. There are often enormous differences between types, each requiring a lengthy syllabus of classroom and simulator training. Commonality is increasing, and in certain instances certification to fly different models is the same, as with the Airbus A330 and A340 or Boeing 757 and 767.

Like everything else in the pilot's world, seniority bidding determines which machine he drives. Transitioning to another model, or upgrading from first officer to captain of the same model, he undergoes the complete training regimen. Even if previously checked-out on a particular plane, a pilot sweats through an extensive requalification program.

I sat next to a pilot who told me he flew out of Miami. When I asked how he liked living in Florida, he replied, "Oh, I live in New Jersey." Please explain.

Many pilots are based, or to use some awful-sounding airline-speak, domiciled, in cities other than those in which they live. For example, a pilot who lives in Boston might actually *work* out of Chicago, and will commute back and forth.

Airlines reassign crews from city to city—bases open and close, aircraft assignments change, etc. To avoid the difficulties of relocating every two years, pilots commonly get a part-time residency called a "crash pad," where they'll stay, if needed, during work rotations. (The décor and sanitary standards of the average crash pad are a topic for another time. I once rented an apartment with six other pilots that we divided up with sheets of dirty plywood.) Others, when it's affordable, purchase hotel rooms on a nightly basis. A few have been known to sleep in cars.

Commuting dovetails with most pilots' monthly schedules, comprised of multiday assignments lasting anywhere from a single night's layover to a week or more away. Commutes through two or more time zones are not uncommon. Legend has it there was once an Eastern Air Lines captain domiciled in Atlanta but who lived in Wellington, New Zealand.

There is no such thing as a "typical" pilot's schedule, as seniority standing has enormous impact on how often somebody flies, where he flies, and how long he gets to stay there. Having resided on a few seniority lists myself, in both high and low standing, I can wax about three-day layovers at the JW Marriott in Mexico City or four-day stints at the Brussels Hilton. Then again, I get the shakes remembering nine-hour rests at cheap hotels in Lansing, Moline, and Syracuse.

For cabin staff it works similarly. A senior flight attendant might pull the same forty-eight-hour downtime in Athens or Singapore as a senior captain. There are, however, fewer time and duty protections, and bottom-dwellers on the list have it tough. A junior flight attendant will have a more demanding schedule and fewer contractual protections than a junior pilot.

Are the pilots of commuter planes castaways from the big airlines, and/or not skilled enough to fly large jets? Are they simply building experience?

Your basic RJ is no less sophisticated, really, than an MD-80 or 757. Smaller, yes; quaint, no. Those at the controls tend to be younger (though not always) and less experienced (though not always), and many see their job as a stepping-stone. But phrases like "less experienced" and "stepping-stone" foster a misconception that these professionals lack the resume to fly larger equipment.

Everything depends on the hiring trends. Transition to a major airline depends far less on a pilot's aggregate hours than on the volume of jobs available. One is not exiled to the regionals for lack of flight time, necessarily, as much as in deference to the whims of expansion, attrition, and turnover. Tenure at the regionals isn't easy, as the culture tends to err on the abusive side. Schedules range from tedious to backbreaking, and the pay is the kind of thing that causes people to skip their college reunions. During the 1990s it was practice to require new-hires to front their own training costs. After meeting acceptance standards, pilots were required to pay upwards of $10,000 or more for first officer qualification, upon completion of which they could then look forward to a starting salary somewhere in the range of $20,000. Suffering for our art indeed. Expressions like "apprenticeship" and "internship" were tossed around by those who advocated these schemes—something I always found offensive since, by this point on the career ladder, pilots already have paid their dues.

Conditions are improving and today a six-figure income is not unusual for senior captains at companies like American Eagle or Comair, where increasing numbers are staying put. Considering the death rattles from above, they may have little choice, a reality that encourages the ranks to press for better pay and benefits.

Most regionals, even those wholly-owned by a major, are operated independently, with their own seniority groups and collective bargaining agreements. Pilots (and flight attendants too) get a thrill from flying an aircraft that says Delta or United or Northwest on the side, but it's the small print—Connection, Express, Airlink—that counts. They are not entitled to jobs at the majors by virtue of a paint job or code-share affiliation. If a crewmember at SkyWest Airlines, d.b.a. Delta Connection, wants to drive a 767 for Delta, he applies there on his own and hopes for the best, just like anybody else. American Eagle and Continental Express are two exceptions. They've reached agreements whereby limited numbers of pilots are granted flow-through rights.

What about at a discount airline like Southwest or AirTran? Should we be wary? And how about cargo pilots?

Airlines will brag their employees are, in some indefinable way, better than everyone else's, but this is just posturing. While airlines have their specific in-house cultures, it wouldn't be fair, as a general rule, to say a certain caliber of pilot goes to a certain caliber of airline. Competition for jobs is ruthless, even in the headiest boom times. There is virtually never a shortage of evenly qualified resumes, whether at American or AirTran, and much of where a pilot ends up is a function of luck.

Of that, one man's curse is another's fortune. Seniority lists expand and contract, and periods of growth and expansion at one airline are times of red ink, layoffs, and stagnancy at another. Just because Delta's most senior captain makes more than his counterpart at JetBlue, that doesn't mean he will have made more money or enjoyed a better life there during the full course of a career.

Lots of people assume cargo pilots exist on some lower echelon of the skill scale, and while this has some merit with respect to second- or third-tier carriers, nothing is further from the truth at the likes of Federal Express, UPS, and the other bigger names. Pilots do not work here because they lacked the pedigree for United or American. Many prefer the anonymity of the cargo world, away from the crowds and hassles. Pay scales and benefits are roughly on par. There's a certain cachet to be exploited when carrying humans as opposed to boxes, but its value varies from ego to ego.

Another misconception pertains to cargo jets themselves, and I'm partly to blame considering some of the anecdotes I've shared. Although it's true that plenty of freighters are near the ends of their useful lives, a great number are newer ships built expressly for freight. Amidst UPS' thirty-year-old conversions (re-engined and updated with fancy avionics, I should add), are Boeings and Airbuses fresh from the assembly lines. Same story at FedEx and elsewhere.

Aren't most pilots culled from the military?

The split is about 50-50, but differs airline to airline. Some have in-house cultures more traditionally affiliated with the armed forces. So far in my beleaguered career I've worked at two airlines that operate large jets. At one, about 70 percent of the pilots are ex–Air Force, Army, Navy, Marines, or Coast Guard. At the other it's closer to a quarter. At the regionals, the military number tends to be smaller, historically because these pilots skip the regional step on their way to the big leagues. For civilians, regional flying is the experiential equivalent of missions in an F-18 or C-130. Which isn't to say military flyers don't find themselves stuck in the minors. It happens all the time. The hiring trends, again, are in charge.

As to which makes the better aviator, we could spend all day polling and debating and never reach a consensus, either statistically or philosophically. At one company's new-hire class I remember marveling—if that's the proper term—at the military pilots' total unfamiliarity with the basic ins and outs of airline life that I'd been intimate with for years. By that I mean cultural aspects—the ways of paperwork and politics—not actual *flying*. But that's what training was for, and I, by contrast, had never sat in the commander's seat of a C-5 or faced hostile fire. By calling it a wash I'd be flattered.

I'm often asked if there aren't distinctive military and civilian flying styles. Styles of haircut, perhaps, but within an airline, as a rule, no. One customary prejudice that says Navy pilots land one way and Air Force pilots another, owing to methods used on aircraft carriers, but you can chalk this up to friendly bickering between service branches.

I rarely come across female airline pilots. What discourages women from becoming pilots, and is there a culture within the industry that keeps women from flying for the airlines?

I'm unsure what discourages women from becoming pilots in equal number with men, though I assume they'd be the same things that discourage them from other male-dominated roles and vice versa.

By the mid 1990s about 3 percent of all cockpit crewmembers in the United States were women—a total of about 3,500, representing a thirty-fold increase since 1960. That number has fallen sharply with ongoing job cuts and industry reshuffling. "Most women pilots are junior," says Captain Jessica Stearns of the International Society of Women Airline Pilots, alluding to those unstable lower portions of seniority lists. "The last number I saw was 1 percent."

Certain airlines are especially well known—perhaps notorious is the right word, depending on which disgruntled male pilot you're talking to—for recruitment of women. Before the meltdown, United Airlines was home to about 500, the highest number at any large airline in the world. Affirmative action–style recruitment incites the same controversy in aviation as in other fields: Women are sometimes accepted with fewer qualifications than competing males, a policy that, while not unsafe (all candidates meet minimum requirements and endure the same training), raises the ire of more experienced men who've struggled to land a job and were passed over.

The Organization of Black Airline Pilots reports a maximum of 675 African-Americans working for U.S. airlines, including fourteen women (eight of them at United).

You told us landings are sometimes purposely crooked or firm, and the smoothness of a landing is not a legitimate way for passengers to gauge a pilot's skill. What, then, *is* an accurate yardstick?

I suggest there isn't one. And to take this another step: Regardless of whether a touchdown is purposely *or* accidentally firm, a flight should no more be judged by its landing than the success of organ transplant surgery is judged by the alignment of the sutures. Facets of skill, technique, and knowledge are obviously brought to bear numerous times on a given flight, but this happens in an exceptionally complex and dynamic environment. Indicators of competence are not the kind of thing a passenger in row 14 can pick up on, and I recommend you not appraise pilots through the jigs, turns, and bumps that occur while aloft.

A particular angle of bank might seem capriciously steep, or a landing might be clumsy, but any number of operational factors could be at hand, and things like this make lousy criteria. The severity of a maneuver, whether perceived or actual, is not always a crewmember's whim or lack of finesse. Within an airline, all pilots are taught the same methods and will fly the same procedures at roughly the same angles, rates, and speeds. When vagaries of technique or personality do manifest themselves, it's not in a way—say "going too fast" or "turning too sharply"—that a passenger is able to sense. And while I don't intend to belittle your powers of observation, remember that perceptions are strongly influenced by nervousness or lack of understanding. Pilots will encounter post-flight critiques like, "Hey, how come you descended so rapidly back there?" when in fact the descent was perfectly tame.

This will lead to a discussion of pilot error. Defensive as this nastily ambiguous expression makes me, the notion of pilots screwing up is not to be scoffed at. Yet even the most ostensibly cut-and-dry offenses turn out to be affairs of complicated extenuation, and they rarely have anything to do with overly steep turns, too-rapid descents or bumpy landings. So you can, at least, put away your image of the cowboy airman hot-rodding his passengers to doom.

When things go bad, pilots do more or less what they *have* to do, so there isn't a lot of room for talent to save the day. Luck is a bigger factor. Which isn't a knock on, for example, Captain Al Haynes and his crew, who gallantly crash-landed their DC-10 in Iowa in 1989 after an engine explosion bled the plane of its vital hydraulics. Most pilots would have done the same thing with, give or take, the same results. I'll get shouted down for saying that, as everyone loves a hero, but it's true. Diametric to successes like that of Haynes are some disgraceful mistakes, but the quantity of negligence, the act alone, usually isn't proportionate to the subsequent carnage. Ought we judge the crime by body count, or the nature of the infraction? Captain Jacob van Zanten of the Dutch

747 at Tenerife misunderstood a takeoff clearance—not the rarest sin in the world—and 583 people paid the price.

Pilot seniority affects pay, the type of plane he flies, and so on. Therefore, should one extrapolate that larger planes on the longest routes are operated by the safest, most experienced pilots?

Not really. For one thing, a pilot's experience level, measured by the fatness of his logbook or the grayness of his hair, does not invariably equate to a higher level of knowledge or skill. All pilots are trained and held to equal standards.

The seniority thing is complicated, as pilots bid their choices according to schedule, where they wish to live, and so forth, and are not always lured to the heavier metal. There's no "graduating," so to speak, from smaller planes to larger ones. Quality of life might be better on a 737 than a 777, even if pay scales favor the latter. So, a senior pilot might opt for short-range domestic flying, allowing somebody more junior to hold long-range international. This works not only for aircraft assignments, but for seat position as well. Bypassing an upgrade to captain isn't the least bit unheard of. Life as a senior first officer might be considerably more relaxed than life as a very junior captain.

Thus, a given captain may in fact be *less* experienced, in terms of total flight time, and very possibly younger, than his first officer. That might surprise you, but as a safety factor it means little or nothing.

I find it hard to believe the September 11 skyjackers, taught only as private pilots, were able to steer those Boeings into their targets. What qualitative and quantitative differences are on hand when operating an airliner versus a private plane?

It depends what's meant by "operating." Certain individuals proved—and not to this pilot's surprise—that basic flying skills are enough to drive an already airborne 767 into a skyscraper. Rudimentary climbs, descents, and turns are nothing a competent private pilot couldn't handle at the helm of a Boeing. They'd be messy, but perfectly survivable. But landing that airplane, operating its subsystems, or navigating across great distances, is a different story. The importance of a hands-on "feel" (yes, some pilots are better than others in the innate talent department) versus the acquired knowledge of the specific workings of a particular plane, is something we can debate, but a proficiency in both is required.

In any modern cockpit you'll notice vestigial similarities even to the *Spirit of St. Louis*. At the same time, one glance is a serious dose of technological intimidation. A working knowledge of all those switches, dials, screens, and keypads becomes more crucial as the breadth of the task expands. Are we handling a problem? Is the weather foul? Managing a flight—and managing is such the right word—is a great deal more than straight-and-level steering of the ship. Messing with gravity is the easy part.

It doesn't shock me that the September 11 cabal's feats did not require in-depth technical knowledge or knack. They were out of their league, obviously, but maintaining essential up-down, left-right control was not an overwhelming demand, nor was navigating toward New York in clear conditions. Mohammed Atta and at least one other of his group did buy several hours of simulator training, from a private academy in Florida, on a Boeing 727. This was not the same jet used in the attacks (757s and 767s), but it really didn't need to be. Additionally they attained manuals and videos, widely available from aviation suppliers and bookdealers.

They needed some luck, and they got it, with particular regard to flight 77 and the Pentagon. Hitting a stationary target from above at high speed—even a big one with five beckoning sides—is difficult. To make it easier, alleged pilot Hani Hanour did not come in at a steep angle, but "landed" into the building obliquely. These were not show-quality aerobatics; if he'd flown the same profile ten times, half of them he'd probably have tumbled short of the target or overflown it entirely.

Much has been made about the incredible realism in commercially sold desktop simulators—products like Microsoft's Flight Simulator. Around for twenty years, these software games have become so advanced that users learn to manipulate the controls and computers of a jetliner without ever leaving the house. Might their sophistication abet the cause of terrorism?

There's plenty of mettle in a discussion about the increased computerization of airflight technology, but in the connection to terrorism it turns tabloid. With a Gateway and a credit card somebody can learn the basics—and more—of a jetliner's operation. And a trip down the software aisle, or a wade through the inventory at Google, can give you what it takes to build bombs, mix poisons, perform veterinary surgery, or speak Urdu. How unwilling we are to harvest the strange fruits of postmodern technological evolution. On one hand we extol the world-saving glory of our gadgets and gizmos, while at the same time we're chasing down the genie and looking for witches.

In a computer class in college, a professor smugly told us, "airplanes are capable of flying themselves," including takeoffs, cruising, and landing. He maintains the pilots are merely "overpaid fail-safe devices, there to make the passengers feel safe." Is the concept of pilotless planes really viable?

Right around the corner, along with doctorless hospitals and lawyerless courtrooms. We already have machines that help with certain operations, so how far can we be from having a computer perform a heart valve replacement?

That's a flip retort, but the professor is doing the same thing. He is being disingenuous (and he hasn't seen the paychecks of many pilots). In keeping with the habit of those ensconced in technology, he speaks to idealistic devotion to his silicon wafers while more or less oblivious to the boundless contingencies of flight—things that no electric box can be wired to appraise *(see software, page 215)*. Chatting gate-side with a frequent flyer, a pilot hears, "But do you really *do* anything? Doesn't the autopilot do all the flying?" Next time a person lays out an elaborate Thanksgiving dinner, try this: "But did you really *do* anything? Doesn't the *oven* do all the cooking?"

Some will argue that much of the idea is already within the realm of existing technology, and that's true. But much is not nearly enough. As it stands today, planes can and do perform autoland procedures, and have for thirty years. Impressive, but if I went on to describe the knowledge and expertise needed for coordinating and monitoring this "fully automatic" landing, I would write for ten pages.

The military uses unmanned aerial vehicles (UAVs) all the time. These small, remotely-controlled planes engage in reconnaissance, scouting, and even combat missions. For now, their accident rate is about fifty times that of a piloted fighter. The feasibility challenges are awesome. For pilotless flying to become day-to-day would be a huge—and hugely expensive—undertaking with many years of research and immense infrastructure replacement. If you'll allow me to get juvenile for a minute: It's hard enough to get the little trams that take you around DFW or Atlanta to work right, and they're on *tracks*.

Pilots may now qualify to carry cockpit firearms. Are pilots and guns a good mix?

This ongoing controversy inevitably, if annoyingly, gets back to an exploitable postulate about September 11: that armed crews could have prevented the skyjackings and will thwart future ones. A majority of pilots, with support of their largest union, the Air Line Pilots Association, believes so firmly, and embarked on a full-throttle campaign to legislate flight deck sidearms. Effective April 20, 2003, months of lobbying paid off when pilots began carrying handguns for the first time. As of that day, forty-four had graduated from a government-certified course and became Federal Flight Deck Officers, with more to follow. Surveys show about 70 percent of pilots are in favor of the program, though it's doubtful that many will actually participate.

One must admit that in the confines of a cabin aloft, far removed from the nearest police station or call for help, there exists a precarious vulnerability. Yet the idea of an airline employee, even one with a combat background entrusted to operate jet aircraft, appropriating the role of policeman does not sit well with everybody.

Some argue that a fortified cockpit, perhaps augmented with a cabin-view camera, is the better choice. Pakistan International, one of the more security-fixated airlines (possibly with good reason) has installed cameras and bulletproof doors with electronic locks. But the flight deck is not, and never should be, a sealed capsule. Pilots emerge for rests or to use the toilets; flight attendants and other personnel come and go. The potential will always exist for somebody to gain unwelcome admission. Hardly a month after September 11, a deranged man rushed the cockpit of an American Airlines 767, forcing the plane into a dive before he was subdued.

In a way, the issue leads back to passenger screening down on the concourse. Staff at major airports failed to detect smuggled weapons nearly a quarter of the time in tests. Ease of sneaking guns onto airplanes propounds the need for a matched response. Sky marshals are useful here, but with 27,000 flights taking off each day across America, it's foolish to expect a marshal on every plane. Deputized pilots would offer added protection.

Crews, too, would take advantage. Right now, pilots are among the very few airline employees subjected to the comical rigors of the x-ray belt and metal detectors. Captains entrusted with hundreds of lives and aircraft worth hundreds of millions of dollars are asked to hand over their Leatherman tools and open their bags. "Stripped defenseless," as ALPA puts it. "Forcing us to cooperate with terrorists." Histrionic for sure, but the idea of on-duty pilots undergoing pat-downs and underwear inspection is imbecilic. Bypassing this nonsense would, in turn, speed up the process for everyone.

Concerns have been raised over the dangers should gunfire erupt during cruise. The idea of a bullet puncturing a fuselage conjures up Hollywood scenes of screaming passengers disappearing through holes. Actually, such possibilities have been overemphasized. A small caliber hole in an airplane will not, in all likelihood, cause it to crash. A round piercing important equipment, or shattering a window, could be hazardous, but any circumstance grave enough to bring about use of a weapon in the first place, it has to be assumed, options an even worse conclusion.

Some say nonlethal ammunition or stun guns are a safer option. Others disagree strongly. "The only effective response to a lethal threat is lethal force," voices an ALPA official. "Stun guns just aren't up to the job, period. And presence of one implies we're encouraging pilots to deal with air rage incidents, and that's totally false."

Importantly, guns will not be used to break up squabbles or scare unruly passengers into submission. Explains a pilot, "Our jurisdiction will be only in the cockpit." While episodes of air rage indeed are potentially dangerous, brandishing a weapon is to be an absolute final line of defense, with no lesser purpose than to *save the airplane*.

Yet that's where the trouble begins.

Without access to a locked and secure cockpit, the most likely terrorism scenario involves a hostage-taking in the cabin. Is the crew to engage in a gun battle to save lives? Not according to the rules of the tender, but at what point might a pilot open fire, perhaps engaging a lone attacker in a firefight? To save the life of a flight attendant? A child? What if passengers are being executed?

Attempts at gallantry could be hard to resist, and it's not inconceivable that use of a gun could be less of a last-ditch measure of desperation than was intended. This puts me on a slippery slope, and I'll be accused of questioning a pilot's ability to follow his training when things get hot. But what, objectively, defines last-ditch? Are we saving the airplane, or *probably* saving the airplane?

And while persistent security breaches are cause for alarm, do we hand a critical new responsibility to pilots, sky marshals, or both? How many guns are too many? Is the prospect a bit of literal and figurative overkill?

Finally there exists the possibility, however remote, of purloined weapons turned against their owners, or rogue crewmembers turning guns on one another or themselves. At least two disasters were allegedly pilot suicides—EgyptAir flight 990, and a Silk Air 737 in Indonesia. Neither pilot used, or even needed, a firearm, but the presence of one could expedite a deadly temptation.

At ALPA, 73 percent of members give their blessings. Interestingly, this roughly three-quarter split can be traced cynically, if not scientifically, along opinions and ideals that exist *outside* the workplace. Casual queries portray an almost uncanny break along political and cultural lines. Those most eager to carry pistols seem to be the meat-eating, right-leaning types; those more hesitant tend to be less aligned with, shall we say, the more fiery and rhetorical aspects of patriotism.

As a group, airline pilots aren't generally known for subtlety or abstraction. The business has its closet intellectuals and bookish types, but your average pilot is more likely a NASCAR fan with a suburban ranch house than the kind of guy who relaxes in a turtleneck reading *The New Criterion*. There *is* a curious ideological undercurrent that betrays the matter as one less of safety and more of emotion. Hardly all Democrat pilots are peaceniks, of course, and hardly all Republicans are gun zealots. But to ignore the culture question is doing the debate a disservice. Who is driving the cause, and why, is important.

ALPA has worked to distance itself from a splinter group that has seized on the issue as a Second Amendment add-on. Still, in the union's call to arms, its typically articulate and well-reasoned opinions occasionally dip into cowboy blather. ALPA's website proclaimed of the mix of pilots and pistols, "A deterrent to terrorists and crackpots that believe breaching the cockpit is a freebie in America."

Stick that in your pipe, Osama.

Ultimately, the kernel of the argument isn't one of patriotic posturing, shattering windows, or the sovereignty of a flight deck. Rather, how useful is the idea in the first place? Are we giving valuable time and money to a red herring? Are we pandering to a hunger for *perceived* safety? In the meantime, pilots will have to be trained and retrained; procedures and regulations will need draft and approval. All of this, to some extent, detracts from an airlines' foremost mission, which is not law enforcement or the oversight of firearms inventories.

Arming pilots is not a bad idea so much as a less crucial one than all the talk implies. Pilots, their unions, the FAA, and the airlines have more to worry about than crackpots invading the cockpit. It wasn't a gun that kept Richard Reid and his explosive sneakers from bringing down a fifth plane just before Christmas 2001. The likelihood of another kamikaze-style attack has been greatly reduced, and other areas of security deserve equal time, debate, and political capital.

At the risk of tempting another fist clenching testimonial on the dastardly deeds of September 11, I wince, just so slightly, at how much attention this issue manages to draw. If nothing else we should keep things as voluntary as possible and away from government mandate. Allowing pilots to partake at their choosing, under some grueling rules and supervision, limits the scope and cost of what is, in the end, a somewhat relevant safeguard.

What is the purpose of the complicated watches I always see pilots wearing? And what do you carry in those black bags?

The purpose of the watches is to tell us what time it is. Those gaudy little devices are an essential part of our uniform, perhaps in tribute to the days when goggled aviators used gold Rolexes to . . .

I don't know. Watches are required as backups to the ship's clocks, but nothing more elaborate than a sweep hand is needed. My red bezel Swiss Army watch does the job wonderfully.

The bulk of the ubiquitous black flight case is a library of manuals and heavy, leather-bound navigational binders. Inside the binders are hundreds of pages of maps, charts, airport diagrams, and other technical arcana. Unlike those a private pilot might use, they are tailored to specific airlines. The only thing a pilot dreads more than a Chapter 11 bankruptcy is having to collate and insert the constant stream of revisions to these books. The pages are replaced by hand, one at a time. A captain once offered me five dollars for each batch of revisions I took care of for him. If this sounds unnecessarily tedious, it is, and airlines are turning to virtual manuals, equipping crews with laptops and easily updated CDs. The rest of the inventory includes a headset, flashlight, checklists, and pages of company or aircraft-related miscellany. Personal sundries are stickies, pens, calculators, and ramen noodles to be heated in the hotel coffeemaker during those nine-hour layovers.

A popular news story involved a pilot caught napping on a flight from the Bahamas. Is exhaustion a concern? If so, why not allow a pilot to sleep if a second one is present?

If you're hoping for some scandalous eyewitness accounts of crewmembers nodding off over the ocean, you can stop reading. I'll leave that for *Dateline*. Indeed, in the summer of 2003 news magazines went crazy for the amusing story of a pilot caught napping by a passenger's camcorder. The company involved was a tiny, Florida-based airline with a single small turboprop (no, not even a cockpit door). The airline's name doesn't deserve mention because, frankly, the whole thing was ridiculous.

It's my hesitant opinion that pilots be allowed to nap, but the FAA considers the issue radioactive and keeps it off the table. There's also some merit to the idea that forcing two pilots to stay awake diminishes the odds of *both* of them falling asleep.

While a minor issue at the larger airlines, fatigue at cargo carriers, where back-of-the-clock rotations are par, and at lower-rung regionals and charter outfits, where schedules can be punishing, is a concern. Not a major concern, but certainly a more substantial one than pilots smoking crack or shooting heroin. The FAA realizes this, I have to assume, but chooses to put its resources into drug testing and other politically expedient issues with limited economic repercussions. Meanwhile it analyzes NASA studies on circadian rhythms to determine if exhaustion could possibly be a detriment to job performance. In no way am I advocating pilots be allowed to intoxicate themselves in violation of law or common sense, but ask yourself this: Whom would you prefer at the controls of your plane on a stormy night—a pilot who smoked a joint three days ago, or one who had six hours of sleep prior to a twelve-hour workday in which he's flown seven legs? The first pilot has indulged in a career-ending toke; the second is in full compliance with the regulations.

Short-haul domestic schedules are no less fatiguing than long-hauls. A nonstop to Seoul might be physically draining, but at least it's a single shot, with designated rest breaks and the low workload of protracted, high-altitude calm. The up-and-down rigors of Chicago-Indianapolis-Detroit-Cleveland are what expend a crew's strength and acuity. Having done a bit of both, I find intercontinental flying not nearly as enervating as multileg hops. Long-haul flights bring along supplemental pilots to relieve the original crew, who retire to bunks or designated cabin seats. (Certain planes have secluded—and surprisingly spacious—crew rest chambers either above or below deck both for pilots and cabin crew.)

The trouble isn't flight hours, it's *duty* hours. A domestic pilot is held to no more than eight hours aloft on a given day, but when the weather goes bad, that can entail twelve, thirteen, even sixteen hours of actual time on the job, with long stretches of sit-around between takeoffs. Then, on a short-duration overnight, much of your allotted rest is consumed by bookend transport—an hour's trip from the terminal to Holiday Inn—and chasing down food at one a.m.

Regulatory loopholes have been tightened in the past few years, but these small changes didn't come easily. Whenever government tries to take a bite out of this problem, the ATA (Air Transport Association), lobbying arm of the airlines, swings its propaganda apparatus into action. During federal hearings in August 1999, ATA Senior Vice President John Meenan got a storm brewing when he said, "There has never been a scheduled commercial airline accident attributed to pilot fatigue—not one, not ever." A testament to pilots doing a good job under lousy conditions, if you ask me, and not a justification for legally sanctioned somnambulance on the flight deck.

What brought the hearings on was the crash of American Airlines flight 1420, which two months earlier slid off the runway at Little

Rock, Arkansas, during a thunderstorm, killing eleven people, including the captain, who'd been on duty for more than thirteen hours. Investigators partly attributed the incident to crew fatigue. At least two accidents involving cargo jets have been blamed more directly on tiredness.

Clearly this is one of those difficult-to-quantify factors after a crash, and as I said it's more of a cargo-regional-charter phenomenon than the norm at Delta, United, or American, where collective bargaining agreements usually add buffers to the skeletal federal requirements. I've endured lifestyles at airlines at either end of the spectrum. To me, an assignment at the latter is, by comparison, like getting a free day pass to a health spa. Passengers shouldn't feel inclined to, um, lose sleep over the matter.

How do pilots get along with gay flight attendants? I'd expect many macho personalities are prone to clash with those who exhibit effeminacy. And what about gay and lesbian pilots? Any queer people in the cockpit?

Pilot–flight attendant interaction, regardless of personalities or sexual orientations, tends to be terse these days. Cockpit and cabin crews often stay in separate hotels, for instance. But to answer the question, the word I'd go with is *cordial*. Cordial doesn't always mean friendly, but for the most part the interplay is very professional and free of hostility. How much of this is in fear of litigation or getting fired is open to debate, but even that counts for something. You'll hear small doses of sarcasm and fun-poking once the cockpit door is closed, but while I don't suppose that's terribly surprising, it's a lot more tame than you might expect. Many pilots, even the most conservative, can be surprisingly open-minded. Perhaps association with gay coworkers over an extended period of time softens ingrained stereotypes. I've worked with a minimum of four gay or lesbian pilots, including a former military flyer, all exhibiting varying degrees of openness about their sexuality.

Back in the days when flight attendants were called stewardesses and handsome pilots wrestled their airplanes around without fancy computers, movies loved to imply these attractive crews were hopping from bed to bed. With flight attendants looking more matronly and pilots attaining the same level of mystique as rural-town taxi drivers, it's difficult, if not painful, to imagine that there's much hanky-panky still going on. Is there?

If so, I have long been excluded from it. All in all it's no different from any other work environment, though things are faster and looser, which is to say younger, at the regionals. Pilots tend to be straightlaced sorts, which contributes to our collective chastity, but I've heard the same stories from the '60s and '70s as everyone else. Too bad, maybe. Getting laid is a lot more fun than getting laid *off*.

From time to time I'm asked to comment on the 2003 incident in which two Southwest Airlines pilots were terminated for going au naturel in flight. I'm withholding statement since these sorts of things have a way of becoming wildly distorted when stripped, if you will, of context. I don't know what they were doing. And no, I've never taken my clothes off during flight.

Well, except once, in the summer of 1995, when a pavement-melting heat wave was sweeping across the Midwest and I was based in Chicago as a first officer on a sixty-four-seat ATR-72.

The European-built ATR was a wonderful example of technology for the sake of itself—a fragile, gratuitously sophisticated plane deployed on short-range commuter routes that require sturdy, low-tech dependability. And in all that fancy wiring and plumbing, they forgot the air-conditioning. Tiny eyeball vents blew out tepid wisps of air. On this particular day, the temperature had hit 107, and a sickly haze washed over O'Hare like a tide of yellow steam. I was up front, finishing my preflight checks and waiting for the captain. I was so hot that I could hardly move. So, I took my shirt and tie off. Pilot shirts, which are mostly polyester, are uncomfortable enough even in a perfect climate. Crank the heat and it's like wearing chain mail. I also removed my shoes and socks.

The captain arrived—an overweight, slow-moving fellow in his fifties whom I'd never met before. He stepped into the cockpit and discovered Patrick Smith drenched in perspiration, dehydrated, and wearing only his blue pants and a Sony headset. He didn't speak at first. Then he sat down, looked at me, and said quietly: "You *are* going to put your clothes back on, aren't you?"

My answer was no. I told him I'd get dressed again as soon as the inside temperature fell below 95 degrees, provided I was still conscious. I offered to put a T-shirt on, but the only one I could reach, from my hand luggage, was a Hüsker Dü tour shirt, an artifact from 1983. It was almost as discolored as the putrid Chicago sky, and on the front was printed METAL CIRCUS, which seemed only to further discombobulate the captain. "Arright, fine," he said. "Just don't let anyone see you." And so I flew barefoot and bare chested, all the way to Lansing and back.

5

Life in the Cabin

. . .

On a Sunday morning I'm catching Malaysia Airlines flight MH091 from Newark to Dubai, and eventually onward to Kuala Lumpur. Newark, now cloyingly recast as Liberty International Airport, is forever the same old bowl of concrete and cars. In a cheerless restaurant in Terminal B I'm eating breakfast beneath framed pictures of sandwiches when the Malaysia crew comes promenading past, headed for their Boeing 777 at the end of the concourse—the pilots in sharply cut, military-style suits, the stewards in green tuxedoes, the girls in sarong-style dresses of melon and teal.

At the surrounding tables are the rest of flight 91's eventual occupants, and present company excluded it's a substantially . . . let's just say Eastern-looking lot—a mix of Arab and Malay and

Indian, with a liberal distribution of skullcaps and prayer beads, and a handful of women in full black burqa. It's all very glammy and international here in decidedly working-class Newark. I like it, even if it's probably a disconcerting sight for the throngs headed to Detroit and Charlotte, with enough dark skin and beards to keep many Americans away from airports forever and hunkered down in their xenophobic hidey-holes. And while I hate saying it, something tells me MH091 gives a thrice-weekly dose of the willies to the already edgy screeners down at security . . .

After standing in queue for fifteen minutes I approach the metal detectors, where a screener greets me good morning. She is wearing paramilitary-style uniform complete with shoulder braids, combat boots, and a beret. Across her back it reads SECURITY in heavy gold lettering. This is supposed to look and feel like the ordered confidence you'd encounter in Europe or Asia. But the too-sharp creases in the pant's legs, the snapping gum, and the glossy lipstick all expose the phoniness and desperation of the scene. These aren't even the trappings of a third world state—something you'd see at the airport in Quito or Entebbe. They're a carnival imitation of those places, with uniforms straight from an old Monty Python wardrobe.

A fork, part of my normal carry-on inventory for years, is confiscated from my luggage. In a few days that fork, along with thousands of other expropriated bits of metal, will be hauled off in a sealed bin by the local fire department. Reminded that forks are still dispensed with inflight meals, the screener replies tersely, "That's what they want us to do."

Nearby a National Guardsman is flirting with a group of teenagers. Troopers are cracking jokes, bags are toppling from the belt. "Take your shoes off, please." I'm ashamed and embarrassed. Is *this* the new world of flying?

Our zero-tolerance policy toward carrying weapons—perceived or real—has turned the predeparture process into a pageant of humiliation. Airports have become scrap-metal repositories, while thousands of people are asked to remove their shoes because one man, on one occasion, had the idea of concealing explosives in his sneakers. At the risk of sounding flip, are strip-searches to follow? After all, even the stupidest terrorist will see that sneakers are out, and what more fiendish than a bomb in your underwear?

I've heard people recount, "I was not allowed to carry through my coffee without tasting it first. But what if I'd simply filled my shampoo bottle full of gasoline?" The ironies and examples are endless: A shattered wine bottle is just as sharp as a boxcutter; a shiv of snapped-off plastic no less lethal than a knife. And so forth.

The preoccupation with Weapons of Mass Distraction gets back to a stubborn fixation with the September 11 template, assuming any sequel is bound to unfurl around a do-it-yourself arsenal similar to that used by the original nineteen skyjackers. Terrorists, the intercepted messages and payrolled tipsters inform us, are again targeting airliners. But while I don't know exactly what an al-Qaeda operative might have in store, I'm skeptical of one thing, which is the likelihood of another suicide skyjacking. The skyjack model, it's critical to note, is forever changed, as never again will anybody believe a purloined plane is headed to Havana, Beirut, or anywhere but into the side of a building. I can't imagine anybody making it two steps up the aisle, to say nothing of into the cockpit, with less than a bucket of pinless grenades balanced on his head.

If anything, the ongoing nonsense underscores our vulnerability by flaunting our refusal to behave rationally. One is reminded of the movie *Brazil*, Terry Gilliam's 1985 film about a totalitarian state under constant barrage of terrorist bombings, brought to the brink of collapse and hilarity by its own foolish, hyperextended authority. Just imagine a platoon of firefighters carting away a locked container of forks, tweezers, and hobby knives.

In an atmosphere charged with trauma, we've come to view security as a phenomenon of pure cause-and-effect. We're like children in the school playground, who in recounting some lurid tale from the TV news or eavesdropping on some grievous grownup discussion, usually get the facts right but miss the point entirely, failing to scrutinize our opponents' wider intents and purposes. We construe every event, be it mundane or serious, as some glaring weakness in our already overstressed system, outrage erupting every time the next nail file, Popsicle stick, or rubber nose and sunglasses is found lurking in a seat pocket. Even the act of snapping a photograph from a concourse window might earn you a chat with a policeman, a policy that smacks of Iron Curtained Moscow or Bucharest. The cry is always to bolt more doors, deny more access, and concoct more high-tech gadgetry.

I'm unsure which would be the better quotation to drop here, Franklin's famous bit about sacrificing liberty for safety, or maybe something more ornery from H. L. Mencken. Whichever old sage would be more appalled by the goings-on, we're more than happy to empty our pockets, rat out our neighbors, pull down our pants. Enough of us, at least, to keep the beast fed and happy. This is what we want: if it equates to safer flying, or more accurately the *perception* of it, by all means, yes, x-ray my Nikes and take my nail-clippers. The TV cameras and newspapers have quoted us time and time again, acquiescing with a sigh: "Well, it sucks, but if it makes flying safer I'm all for it."

But what if it doesn't?

Neither all the determination in the world, nor the most sweeping regulations we dare codify, will outsmart a cunning enough saboteur. Preferring a path of lesser resistance, terrorists will fight along a moveable and eternally porous front. Even our leaders admit this, yet over and over, even as we languish in security lines to have our luggage and dignity eviscerated, we give in to the notion that just about anything, no matter how illogical, inconvenient, or unreasonable, is justified in the name of safety.

As airplane nuts in junior high school, my friends and I spent virtually every weekend roaming the terminals of Boston's Logan International Airport. I came to know that airport as one learns the way from bedroom to bathroom at 4 a.m. Being kids on the verge of our teens, much of our time there was spent engrossed in pranks and unauthorized snooping. Logan became an amusement park of dastardly challenges. We sauntered through metal detectors, rode carousels through baggage rooms, crawled through hatchways, and sneaked into stairwells. At one point we knew the doorway codes to several secure areas.

Our most cherished activity, though, was gaining access to the airplanes themselves. We'd stake out the gate of an arriving flight, then ask an exiting agent or crewmember if we could take a peek at the cockpit. Cordial captains would give us tours, inside and out, of our favorite planes. On some occasions we were told to go ahead, unsupervised, often by the captain himself. "Just don't monkey around with anything." Or, more daringly, we'd simply stroll down the enclosure and step aboard.

Once, as seventh graders, two friends and I spent more than an hour in the cockpit of a Northwest DC-10, utterly unbeknownst to anyone besides ourselves. A mechanic came aboard for a check and found us in the pilots' chairs, seatbelts on, pretending to be airborne over the ocean somewhere. This was the late 1970s. The threat of terrorism, mind you, was not some nascent fear in the backs of people's minds.

Looking back at my forays at Logan, was security dysfunctional, begging for acts of sabotage? No, not really. In essence it's no different than today. Isn't flying safer than it used to be? Probably, but it was never particularly dangerous to begin with—not thirty years ago, and not the day Mohammed Atta and his henchmen walked aboard with a stash of knives, boxcutters, and mace. Antipodal as it may sound in the current climate, the true deadly weapon on September 11 wasn't anything tactile. It was surprise. The tool of choice, had it been boxcutters, butter knives, or bare knuckles and a shod foot, was effectively unimportant, and we needn't scapegoat airport workers, the FAA, or anybody who wears the uniform of an air carrier.

Lost in the outcry is the realization that incidents of terror are more the inevitable work of statistics and politics than examples of carelessness or incompetence. Just as the War on Drugs will not vanquish the supply of illicit narcotics, the War on Terror will not eliminate the supply of angry radicals. Unable to acknowledge this constructively, our stupor is unrelenting. We're asked to accept some "new reality" of air travel, one in which irritation and fear have become institutionalized, when in fact the risks aren't much different than they were ten, twenty, or thirty years ago.

In spite of these threats, and to a large extent in spite of ourselves, air travel remains safe. My self-interests aside, I'll assure you of the system's integrity. I'd like to say more than "get out there and fly," lest I echo some of the more infantile examples of leadership tossed our way—as if there's nothing more noble or patriotic than spending as much money as possible—but truly my best advice is for the public to overcome its squeamishness.

Perhaps the most valuable lesson to be dug from the rubble of Manhattan is the one we're most afraid of: no system is, or ever will be, foolproof. Sobering, but we could use some cold water. What colder than conceding the more or less unstoppable, hit-em-where-they-ain't resourcefulness of terrorism? Sound, competent security greatly improves our chances, whether against the concoctions of a single deranged individual, or organized terror from the caves of Central Asia. But with the advent of every new technology or pledge of better safeguards, we correspondingly inspire the imaginations of those who wish to defeat us.

Hence it's time to address the terrorism issue systemically. Defusing the rage of angry radicals is a long-term anthropological mission for our leaders, not an excuse to barricade public spaces or subvert civil liberties. An ounce of prevention is worth a pound of Semtex, and there's little to gain by bogging down resources in what amounts to a feel-good fantasy. At best, our implacable quest to protect ourselves makes our exceptionally safe skies that much safer. At worst, it's paranoid overkill undermining both security and freedom.

Economy, business class, first class? Where the hell am I sitting and what's the difference?

To a degree, each of these is open to interpretation, but there are four standard cabins: first class, business class, economy class, and Southwest. Just kidding. Southwest's cabins are actually, um, very nice. There are three: first, business, and economy. The latter is often referred to as coach or tourist. An airline may configure a plane with all three cabins, two of them, or just one. The setups will differ within a fleet. Planes that fly domestically are configured differently from those going international.

The levels of service within a specific cabin also vary with destination. First class on a short flight is very different—with entirely different seats and amenities—from first class on a long-haul. If you've experienced both you'll know what I mean. First class be-tween Miami and Minneapolis, or Madrid and Munich, is very nice, but on the same airline to the Far East it's probably outfitted with fully reclining sleeper seats and your own personal mini-cabin (we'll get to these perks more fully in a minute). In some cases it depends on the exact market. New York-Rio and New York-Tokyo are both of similar duration, but only one might be configured with a top-of-the-line first class.

Virgin Atlantic calls first class "Upper Class," while a China Airlines business cabin is "Dynasty Class." On Alitalia, premium passengers relax in "Magnifica Class." To sweeten the implications of "economy," British Airways sells tickets for "World Traveller" class. BA's business seats used to be "Club Class," but now they're "Club World." Somewhere in the fine print, and in the price, you can figure out which of the traditional subdivisions they're talking about. Others have taken to dividing economy into two sections, one with extra legroom. "Economy Plus" is the idea, though tech-nically it's still, well, coach.

On some intra-European flights, classes are partitioned on short notice according to demand. The seats themselves don't change, but the dividing bulkheads and curtains are slid along tracks. On Air France, economy becomes business by virtue of blocking out the middle seat of a three-abreast block. *Voila*, you've got "Euroconcept."

Delta, Continental, and US Airways are among a number of airlines that no longer offer first class on longer international runs, opting for a jazzed-up business class instead. Continental even came up with something called, in all possible obfuscation, "BusinessFirst." Delta's "BusinessElite" is better than any domestic seat, including domestic first class, but lacks the prestige of what's become customary for intercontinental first class. That is, fully flat beds and other extravagances.

As we grumble over the scourges of the typical economy section, not since travelers slept in private berths in the 1940s have things been so comfortable up front, though definitely in a sleeker, twenty-first-century flavor. Not long ago, a fat leather seat and a doting stewardess were the hallmarks of world-class service. Competition and technology have conspired to bring about some of the most eccentrically luxurious standards ever seen.

On Singapore Airlines 747s, first-class passengers doze in private suites with seventy-six-inch seatbeds and down-filled duvets. On request, cabin staff perform turndown service while customers change into Givenchy pajamas. Before going bust, Swissair showcased an Eames-inspired seat with a dining table. There was a second pull-up chair so a passenger could be joined for dinner. "Urban Sleek" isn't the name of a rap singer, it's what Air Canada themes its refitted cabins, which feature sculpted sleepers with a massage function. British Airways offers 180-degree sleepers even in business class, raising the full-service bar on a wide range of routes, including many head to head with American, United, Continental, and Delta.

At Virgin Atlantic, BA's outrè-trendy competitor, one finds double beds, stand-up bars, and an inflight beauty therapist. There are fourteen phases of "lighting mood" adjusted by the crew. Airlines even compete to outdo one another with the contents of their giveaway amenity kits. On Virgin, a rubber duck is included with the usual creams, balms, and eyeshades.

Instead of plastic earpieces and a bulkhead movie screen, we now have fourteen-inch personal monitors, DVD libraries, and noise-reduction headsets from Bose. You might hear of a plane's "IFE system." That's not lingo for some complicated navigational equipment, but for inflight entertainment system. In this era of increased attention to boredom-absorbing gadgetry, it's now called "IFE." (To pilots, already up to their ears in neotechnical patois, the distinction between cockpit and cabin is becoming blurry.)

It goes without saying, however, that most people aren't riding around on expense accounts, and there are millions who'll never see a first- or business-class seat. Enter the innovations of Virgin, Emirates, BA, Singapore, et al. If you think there's only so much comfort to be wrung from a nine-abreast block in economy, take a ride on Swiss International Airlines (the reborn Swissair), which called upon Recaro GmbH, a German manufacturer of automobile seats, to cast streamlined new economy chairs that add two inches of legroom in every row.

Per passenger, the more frill-intensive airlines spend about nine dollars for economy class catering, and about thirty-five dollars for business or first. Lufthansa, if you can't bear the thought of more pretzels, once gave out ceramic jars of pickled herring.

We often hear a plane described as a widebody. Is this just a generic term? And why are airplane seats so cramped?

You might not find "widebody" in the glossary of the Federal Aviation Regulations, but it's neither an arbitrary distinction nor marketing babble. It's any airliner with more than one aisle bisecting the passenger cabin. A single-aisle plane is known in parlance as a "narrowbody," though the layperson rarely hears this, since, to the public, bigger and wider imply additional comfort and safety. We're stuck with the perception regardless of accuracy. The first widebody, and for now still the widest, was the Boeing 747. The smallest—or thinnest—is the 767. Main deck seating for the Airbus A380 is planned to be ten-abreast, just as you'll encounter on 747s. Elbow-level space will be twelve to fourteen inches greater overall, for about 1.3 additional inches per seat.

Despite a few early exceptions, economy class seat widths and configurations haven't changed, really, since the advent of jets. I'm hanging on to my jeans with the thirty-three-inch waist in case I lose those fifteen pounds, and maybe the airlines are thinking the same way. On its record breaking nonstops to Los Angeles and New York *(see longest flights, page 260)*, Singapore Airlines is plucking a seat from every row of its A340-500s, going from eight abreast to seven. Unless you're willing to accept considerably higher fares, though, it'd be foolish to expect most airlines to follow suit on more run-of-the-mill services. That'd be twenty fares sacrificed from a typical narrowbody's economy section. Singapore makes up the difference by expanding its $5000 per head business cabin, called "Raffles Class."

I have less gripe with the width of seats than other ergonomic deficiencies. Sensible and inexpensive upgrades would go a long way toward making a long flight more bearable: footrests, adjustable headrests, and ergonomically shaped armrests. Select airlines have fitted their economy sections with more comfortable, high-tech seats, but alas for we averagely overweight Americans they tend to be outside the United States.

With flight times now surpassing the gestation periods of many small mammals, there are growing concerns about an affliction known as deep vein thrombosis, or DVT, allegedly caused by protracted exposure to the less than spacious confines of most economy seats. Known also as "economy class syndrome," it's a condition where potentially lethal blood clots form in the legs and can spread through the body. To date there's no full scientific consensus as to what extent a plane's cramped quarters contribute to DVT, but those on lengthier trips should avoid remaining sedentary for extended periods. On those megahauls to Singapore, passengers are encouraged to visit the plane's inflight buffet lounge—a stand-up bar and socializing area laid out with snacks, fruit, and beverages. The intent is not only one of diversion, but to entice people to stretch their legs at regular intervals. (For those who wander in barefoot after sleeping, the buffet zone has heated floors).

Please comment on cabin air quality, or lack thereof.

Nobody maintains that the airflow in a pressurized fuselage is akin to an autumn breeze, and the efficacy of ventilation systems varies make to make. Contrary to rumor, however, cabin air is surprisingly fresh and clean. Outside air is blended with recycled cabin air, then routed through hospital quality, microbe-trapping filters. All in all it's no dirtier or more pathogen-laden than you'll find in most enclosed public spaces.

One thing it's *not*, however, is moist, with humidity levels ranging from zero to 15 percent. Because the volume of air is repeatedly exchanged, humidifying a large cabin over the course of a long flight requires elaborate equipment and large amounts of water. One optional humidifying system sells for $180,000 per unit, and even then increases humidity only to 25 percent.

I've heard that pilots decrease airflow to save fuel. And is it true the amount of oxygen is intentionally reduced to keep passengers docile?

While airlines (some of them) are less than spendthrift these days, crews are *not* instructed to reduce circulation to save fuel. Somehow a planeload of pissed-off people negates the benefit of a few leftover gallons of kerosene.

There's no truth whatsoever to the second and more outrageous part of the question. The only way to reduce oxygen in a cabin is to decrease the level of pressurization. Equivalent cabin altitude is held to roughly 5,000–8,000 feet above sea level, depending on cruising altitude and make of the aircraft. Further, a lack of oxygen at high altitude, known medically as hypoxia, might keep you docile, but symptoms also include dizziness, nausea, disorientation, and splittingly painful headaches. A pilot would have to be fairly sadistic to arouse that kind of mass agony. Realize too that the cockpit is not a sealed chamber with its own pressurization system, and it's impossible to tinker with overall oxygen levels without affecting the cockpit. The crew could don its masks, I suppose, but how realistic is it, honestly, to picture the pilots sitting there with oxygen masks on, dialing down the pressurization to partially suffocate the passengers?

Why can't I use my cell phone during flight, and why are laptops also restricted? Even more annoying, we are asked to turn off portable CD players. Can these things really interfere with anything?

The rules are not arbitrary or a scam to make you splurge on pricey onboard satellite phones. In several cases devices—mainly cellular phones—have allegedly meddled with airliner electronics. Chances are you could chat all day and not cause a nuisance, but that doesn't cut it as a regulatory standard.

Cockpit hardware and software use radio transmissions for a number of tasks—talking to controllers, broadcasting transponder information, following ILS guidance for landings. Even if not actively connected, a cell phone's power-on mode dispatches bursts of data that can garble signals. One report cites a regional jet that made an emergency landing after a fire warning sounded. Investigation revealed the alarm was triggered by a ringing cell phone in the luggage compartment.

Skeptics have said, "But on those September 11 planes, many people made frantic calls with no harm to the aircraft." True, but interference would not be readily evident in the cabin, and maybe not the cockpit either. It's not as though you hit SEND and the airplane flips upside down or is yanked off course. The trouble is liable to be subtle, brewing within the electronic melange of cockpit paraphernalia, and not overtly noticeable even to the crew.

There's little evidence that laptop computers pose much threat, though a poorly shielded laptop can, in theory, transmit harmful energy. The airlines are erring on the safe side. And like any other carry-on, computers have to be stowed during takeoff and landing not solely to preclude signal trouble, but to prevent them from becoming 200-mile-per-hour projectiles. Devices like Walkman or Discman players are likewise prohibited during takeoff and landing so passengers are able to hear announcements and instructions in the event of an emergency. In this spirit, maybe the FAA should demand earplug removal and waking up of all sleeping passengers, but for now they've drawn the line at CDs.

On every flight there are dinging sounds that come through the announcement system. Is this a signaling device for the cabin crew?

Yes, and every airline has its own rules for how many dings mean what. It's the likes of "We'll be landing soon, so get the cabin ready." Another series of chimes tells the attendants when the plane has passed through a certain altitude—10,000 feet in most cases—meaning they now may contact the cockpit without fear of interrupting a critical phase of flight.

The cabin crew announces, "Ladies and gentlemen, we have been cleared to land, so please be sure . . ." How can the runway be clear of other planes when we're still several minutes away? And how do the flight attendants know?

It's not, and they don't. The cabin crew has no idea when the flight has been cleared to land—an event that may take place many miles out or only seconds prior to touchdown. Another one you'll hear is "We've begun our final approach . . ." To a pilot, "approach" is a technical term referring to the execution of a published arrival pattern, and *final* approach can mean a couple of different things, both quite specific, pertaining to distance or angle from the runway. Flight attendants use these words generically for convenience.

In the meantime, it is not true that a runway must be vacant for a flight to receive landing clearance. Airplanes are cleared to land all the time when arriving or departing flights are still on the strip. It simply means they may go ahead and land without further communication. If the runway is not eventually vacant, the clearance will be canceled.

As a nervous traveler I'm constantly trying to read the facial expressions of the crew. Is it general policy to not inform passengers of emergencies to avoid panic? I would like to know if death is imminent. Will I see it in the flight attendant's eyes?

Many people expect nothing less than compulsive deception at the hands of the airlines, and carriers themselves have helped breed this. While they've got some work to do in the articulation department, there are no official concealment policies. That said, a crew will not, generally, inform passengers of minor malfunctions with no real bearing on safety: "Ladies and gentlemen, this is the captain. Just to let you know, we've received a failure indication for the backup loop of the smoke detection system in the aft cargo compartment." Being blunt about every little problem invites unnecessary worry, not to mention embellishment. In this example, passengers come home with, "Oh my god, the plane was on fire." Not that your average person isn't bright enough to figure out what is or isn't dangerous, but you're dealing with jargon and terminology that begs to be misunderstood.

There isn't much in the imminent death realm that can go on behind the scenes, with distressed crewmembers pacing the aisles and whispering to each other in secret. If it helps, go ahead and look back at past accidents, and you'll see that things almost never unfold this way. If there is something to worry about, chances are it will be obvious to everyone on the plane. (Note: That does not give you reason to scream or start reciting the Lord's Prayer if there's a compressor stall or rough turbulence.) That glazed look in the flight attendant's eyes is probably one of exhaustion, not fear. And with sabotage lurking in everybody's minds these days, don't be surprised if your overly intensive staring at a crewmember earns you some overly intensive staring right back.

On some flights the audio system has a channel through which I can hear communications between pilots and controllers. I always found this enthralling, but often it's switched off.

At United Airlines, one of the few purveyors of this oddly intriguing form of entertainment, this is called "channel nine" in honor of its position in your armrest dial. It's either fascinating or tediously indecipherable, depending on your level of infatuation with flight. It is often unavailable, at the crew's discretion, because of the unfriendly letters people send and the litigation they threaten when it's perceived the pilots have made some "mistake." Also, passengers not familiar with the vernacular may misinterpret a transmission and assume nonexistent or exaggerated troubles. Let's say a controller is spacing a series of aircraft and asks, "United 537, um, do you think you can make it?" This is a query pertaining to whether a plane can hit a specific height or speed at a specific time or place. Depending on the controller's intonation—or the pilot's reply, "No, we can't make it"—such innocuous exchanges might have a passenger bursting into tears and picturing his wife and children.

In the late 1970s, riders on American Airlines' DC-10s were entertained by a live-action video feed from the cockpit during takeoff and landing. Nowadays some airlines show the view from a nose-mounted camera.

What's with those flight attendant briefings? Why all the gibberish? And what about those safety cards in the seat pockets? They are impossible to understand and nobody looks at them.

In America, commercial flying is governed by a vast tome known as the Federal Aviation Regulations, or FARs. The FARs are an enormous, frequently unintelligible volume that proudly shows off aviation's flair for the ridiculously arcane. Of its crown jewels, none is a more glittering example than the safety briefing, a prolix rigmarole so weighed down with extraneous language that the crew may as well be talking Aramaic or speaking in tongues. When riding along as a passenger I used to shoot dirty looks at those who ignored the demo, and even made a point of paying undue attention just to help the cabin staff feel useful. After a while, realizing that neither the FAA nor the airlines has much interest in cleaning up the fatty babble, I stopped caring.

The demo has become pure camp—a performance art adaptation of some legal fine print. Passengers are subjected to the phrase "at this time" on about thirteen occasions. "At this time we ask that you please return your seatbacks to their full upright positions." Why not, "Please straighten your seats?" Or, "Federal law prohibits tampering with, disabling, or destroying any lavatory smoke detector." Aren't those the same things? How can you destroy something without having tampered with it? And so on. All that's really needed is a short tutorial on the basics of exits, seat belts, flotation equipment, and oxygen masks. This should not entail more than a minute or two. With a pair of shears and common sense, the average briefing could be trimmed to about half its length, resulting in a lucid oration that people will actually listen to.

The fold-out cards are supposed to be a graphic transcription of the same predeparture speech. They are, very similarly, an unimaginative nod to government mandate of their content. The talent levels of the artists speak for themselves; the drawings appear to be a debased incarnation of Egyptian hieroglyphs. Like the speech, they ought to be cleaned up and simplified.

Look on the back where it spells out the emergency exit row seating requirements. The rules instructing who can or can't sit adjacent to the doors and red-handled hatches were a controversy for some time, and the result was a new standard in FAR superfluity— an interminable, bafflingly verbose litany packed with enough legal technobabble to set anyone's head spinning. Exit row passengers are asked to review this information before takeoff. A game: Begin reading the exit row nonsense prior to takeoff and see if you can finish by the time you dock at destination. If you're then able to coherently recite even one of the mandated conditions, go treat yourself to a frozen yogurt or a new tie.

Could some crazy person open the emergency exits or doors in flight?

No. The smaller hatches are restricted by the outward-pushing forces of the pressurized fuselage. Like a drain plug they open inward, and a person would not be capable of overcoming these forces until the aircraft is depressurized. The larger cabin doors are more complicated. Some operate manually, others mechanically. Secured by a series of locks, they also are subject to outward-acting pressure like the hatches, and sensors that do not allow movement while the plane is pressurized.

You'll notice that on the flat shelf portion of the door—so alluring as a resting spot while waiting for the lav—it often says DO NOT SIT. While I wouldn't recommend it, you could probably sit there all day jiggling the handle to your heart's content without eliciting havoc, though you might break the pressurized seal, causing some horrendous noise, or get a light blinking up front.

The other reason they don't want you sitting there is to avoid messing with the inflatable escape slide that lives in the lower door structure. Coming to the gate, you'll hear attendants announcing, "doors to manual," and "cross-check." They are disarming the automatic function of those escape slides, to keep them from billowing into the Jetway or onto the ground when the doors are opened. "Cross-checking," as it sounds, means one crewmember is verifying that another's equipment is in the right position. Another mysterious call might be "two-L" or "one-R." Those are door designations, front to back and left to right.

In 2003 the rear cargo door of an Ilyushin IL-76 came unlatched during flight over central Africa. More than a hundred people were killed when the resultant decompression pulled them to their deaths. Before you gasp, this was a Russian-built transport designed for the Soviet military. Victims had been sitting unrestrained on the freight-deck floor.

Why do I have to open my window shade for landing? And why are the cabin lights dimmed?

You are asked to raise your shade so you can see through the window. Not for the view, but to help you remain oriented if there's an accident. It allows you to keep track of which way is up, and lets you see any exterior hazards—fires, debris—to avoid during an evacuation. Additionally it lets light into the cabin and makes it easier for rescuers to see inside. Dimming the lights is part of the same strategy. Burning brightly, the glare would make it impossible to see outside. And by preadjusting your eyes, you're not suddenly blind while dashing for the doors in darkness or smoke. The emergency path-lighting and signs also will be more visible.

Why am I asked to store my tray table for takeoff and landing, and why is it required to have the seatbacks in their "full upright position"?

Your tray must be latched so that, in the event of an impact or sudden deceleration, you don't impale yourself on it; plus it allows a clear path to the aisle during an evacuation. The restriction on seat recline provides easier access to the aisles, and also keeps your body in the safest position during an impact. It lessens whiplash-style injuries by reducing the distance your head would travel backwards and prevents you from "submarining" under the seat belt.

Keep your belts low and tight. Nothing is more aggravating than hearing a passenger voice the theory that should a crash occur they are guaranteed to perish, so what's the point? Not all accidents are headline catastrophes, and statistically most include survivors. Something as simple as a properly buckled belt could mean the difference between serious and minor injury.

The airlines require purchase of a second ticket so infants can ride in car seats. Is this really necessary? I can't find any statistics on babies injured on airplanes.

Government records inform us that at least three unrestrained children under two years old have died since 1989 in accidents that included survivors. If you want to play the lottery and hold a baby in your lap, that's your call. Your ability to do so is, in a way, a touching bit of libertarian freedom in an otherwise hyper-regulated environment, bolstered by the improbability of anything happening. But is it safe, inherently? No, in fact it's *extremely* dangerous, and it's tough to swallow how the FAA demands carry-ons be tucked away securely yet allows human infants to go unrestrained. Their logic says parents might opt to drive rather than fly if forced to buy an extra seat, and the overall number of deaths would rise through traffic accidents (automobiles are the number one killer of kids under fourteen).

The FAA might change its mind, and a proposal to require child restraint seats is under review. A final ruling will be many months away, probably not before you're reading this, and rest assured parents, not the airlines, will be asked to supply the properly-dimensioned and guideline-approved seats. Airlines want neither the liability nor the logistical outlay a mandate would entail. Before you scoff, remember that your Subaru or Range Rover didn't come with a child seat either. One carrier, Virgin Atlantic, sees it otherwise. Virgin supplies custom seats and does not allow parents to use their own. This is the kind of broad-minded gesture that has made Virgin famous, but they are a small airline whose policy would not translate well at an airline ten or twenty times the size.

Farewise, an infant in a car seat or other restraint is taking up a cushion just like anyone else and therefore, the logic says, does not deserve a free ride. It's been suggested that bulkhead-mounted safety seats be available for a smaller fee than a standard ticket. This is untenable when you consider the liability issues of unattended children and the potential for chaos during an evacuation as people rush to grab their kids. Several non-U.S. carriers equip their planes with bulkhead bassinets for use en route.

How are pets treated below deck? I've heard they are kept in unheated, unpressurized sections of the plane.

At 35,000 feet the outside air temperature is about 60 degrees below zero, and there is not enough oxygen to breathe. Even worse than economy class. Transporting animals in these conditions would not please most customers, especially those who actually like their pets. Yes, the underfloor holds are pressurized and heated. Controlling the exact temperature in these compartments is not always easy, depending on the airplane type and especially during hot weather. The holds can heat up substantially during ground operations, and for this reason some airlines embargo pets for the summer months.

What are some ways in which passengers can make the crew's job eas-ier? And is it helpful to speak up if something doesn't look or sound right? Is it even possible that a passenger could discover danger the crew is unaware of?

There's not much you can do for the sake of the pilots, save leaving your weapons and suicidal tendencies at home, but to help out cabin staff and fellow passengers, here are two recommendations, common sense as they seem: Please don't stand in the aisle during the boarding process surveying the dimensions of the overhead bin. Yes, it should be larger, and no, the man sitting next to you won't mind if you move his raincoat. Stow your things quickly and move into your row. And when possible, use an overhead compart-ment *close to your assigned seat.* Try not to shove belongings in the first compartment you come to. Doing so, you'll fill up the forward bins and people will be forced to seek compartments *behind* their rows. After landing, they must then travel backwards down the aisle to retrieve things, which clogs the deplaning process.

You might also wish to consider sedating or muzzling your in-fant or small child, though I don't think I'm allowed to make this recommendation in professional guise. The incessant, high-pitched shrieking of a baby is even more discomforting than finding a live grenade in your seat pocket.

Customers pass along safety concerns all the time, and never once have I known a pilot to sneer at anybody's well-intended in-quiry. The only time crewmembers take offense is when it's done arrogantly, such as when a guy pokes his head into the cockpit and mumbles, "Hey, your tire's flat," and then walks off. (Of course, the tire is *not* flat.) As this book should testify, most pilots are grateful for a chance to elaborate on a technical matter or discredit some irritating fable.

6

. . . Must Come Down:
Disasters, Mishaps, and Fatuous
Flights of Fancy

. . .

EN ROUTE ANGST AND THE PSYCHOLOGY OF FEAR

Passengers will ask pilots if they're ever frightened; do they consider the possibility that the next flight could be their last? This always has struck me as both a profound and asinine question. "Yes," I'll answer. "Of course I am scared. I am *always* scared." You can take that with the wink it deserves, but nonetheless it contains a nugget of truth, and if I were in your position I'd choose a pilot like me over a nerves-of-steel doubter any day.

People wonder what the single most difficult and stressful aspect of a pilot's job really is—something I can only address in the negative. This is the stuff of divorce and high blood pressure: short layovers in noisy hotels, hour-long waits for a shuttle bus at midnight, schlepping through terminals with forty pounds of gear, hoping to catch a standby seat on the next overbooked departure.

Reaching the flight deck, buckled into his natural habitat, a pilot feels about as much stress as he does when he's kicked back on a leather sofa in front of the TV.

Exaggeration? Somewhat, and importantly so. A pilot's job, after all, is the management of *contingency*. Fires, explosions, physics gone bad, all the nasty scenarios the simulator instructors love. It's all there, coiled beneath the instrument panel, waiting to spring. Theoretically, at least, in a game of comfortable, but never comfortable enough, odds. And the pilot's role is to spring right back. Do pilots worry about crashing? Not in the way of gruesome fantasy or phobic angst, no. As a matter of practicality, of course they do. That's their job.

Can I cure *your* fear of flying? That depends more on the nature of your fears than my skills of explanation. Either way you'll have to trust that I have sympathy for the white knuckler. The ill-at-ease flyer does nothing to enhance the merriment or livelihood of the crew, and in many ways it injures a worker's pride if he is unable to ameliorate your nervousness. The catch is, pilots aren't qualified to psychoanalyze wavering, ambiguous fears of undefineable situations, i.e., "I feel the plane is going to fall from the sky." Propositions of calamity are nothing new to me—I've heard them all from randomly snapping wings to spontaneous plunges to watery doom.

After the 2001 terror attacks, the airlines saw a passenger dropoff approaching 20 percent. Much of that portion has returned, but it's obvious they're more anxious than ever. What if?

Shoulder-fired missiles, terror alerts, armed pilots, and so forth. Should you, the passenger, be worried? Even under worst-case conditions, which is basically where we're at, I'll offer you a solid no. It depends if you're the type who takes the lottery seriously or worries about lightning.

Bill James, the baseball academic, likes to say, "Never use a number when you can avoid it." Normally he's right, and I don't enjoy dishing out numerical platitudes. We're so used to abstract validation of air safety that it no longer makes us *think*. I'll choose something like this, which you can almost visualize: Each day in the United States more than 27,000 commercial flights take to the air. (There are no official worldwide summaries, but extrapolation yields about 50,000 daily trips.) That's every day, every week, every month. The ten most popular airlines alone make over five million flights per year. Of these, the number failing in their attempt to flout gravity can be totaled in extremely short shrift. During 2002, not a single fatality was recorded among America's airlines. It's not always so impressive, but it's always close.

In a 2003 study published by *American Scientist* magazine, University of Michigan researchers Michael Flannagan and Michael Sivak reevaluated the old flying-versus-driving contention. To be as conservative as possible, their technique calculated probabilities based not on kilometers covered, but on numbers of takeoffs and landings, when over 90 percent of air crashes occur. And they considered highway data only from rural interstates—the *safest* driving environment. Their data showed that if a passenger chooses to drive, rather than fly, the distance of a typical flight segment, he is sixty-five times more likely to be killed. Flannagan and Sivak conclude: "For flying to become as risky as driving, disastrous incidents on the scale of those of September 11 would [have to occur] about once a month."[1]

If somebody is threatening to fly a jet into the Eiffel Tower, does that mean flying is dangerous? No, if anything—and that's not saying much—it means the Eiffel Tower is dangerous. While I sense that I'm naïve for asking you to behave in strict deference to the odds, I'm afraid that's the most meaningful thing I can do. So splash some cold water on that television. Your enemy is the scaremonger and his seed of fear, as much as any skulking terrorist, exploding engine, or jolt of turbulence.

What are the ten worst air crashes of all time?

While not to disaffirm the spirit of what you've just read, even the most uptight flyers grow bored from monotonous reminders and analogies about the safety of flying. In a nod to those annoyed by statistical platitudes and brave enough to indulge your morbid curiosities, I'll present the following catalog. Tastefully and educationally, of course.

One could argue the World Trade Center attacks deserve top billing. However, the planes-as-weapons phenomenon changes

[1]Michael Flannagan and Michael Sivak. *American Scientist*, Jan-Feb 2003, Vol. 91 number 1.

things, and to include the twin tower implosions here would be a blatant stretch, no less than a Cessna detonating a bomb over a crowded city could qualify as an "air disaster." (A turboprop once plowed into a crowded market in Zaire killing more than three hundred people, only *two* of whom were on the airplane.) To level the field, perhaps we should remove *all* on-the-ground casualty figures from crash totals. This seems the fairest method by which to compare accidents, and is something everyone who compiles air safety data should consider. Until then, the list goes like this:

1. *March 27, 1977.* Two Boeing 747s, operated by KLM and Pan Am, collide on a foggy runway at Tenerife, in Spain's Canary Islands, killing 583 people. Confused by instructions, KLM departs without permission and strikes the other jet as it taxies along the runway.

2. *August 12, 1985.* A Japan Air Lines 747 crashes near Mt. Fuji on a domestic flight, killing 520. The rupture of an aft bulkhead, which had undergone faulty repairs following a mishap seven years earlier, causes destruction of the airplane's tail and renders it uncontrollable. A JAL maintenance supervisor later commits suicide. The airline's president resigns and accepts full, formal responsibility, visiting victims' families to offer a personal apology.

3. *November 12, 1996.* An Ilyushin IL-76 cargo jet from Kazakhstan collides in midair with a Saudia 747 near Delhi; all 349 aboard both planes are killed. The Kazakh crew disobeys instructions, and neither plane is equipped with collision-avoidance technology.

4. *March 3, 1974.* In one of the most gruesome crashes ever, a Turkish Airlines DC-10 goes down near Orly airport, killing 346. A poorly designed cargo door bursts from its latches and the rapid decompression collapses the cabin floor, impairing cables to the rudders and elevators. Out of control, the plane slams into the woods northeast of Paris. McDonnell Douglas, maker of the DC-10, which will see more controversy later, redesigns the cargo door system.

5. *June 23, 1985.* A bomb planted by a Sikh extremist blows up an Air India 747 on a service between Toronto and Bombay. The plane falls into the sea east of Ireland, killing 329. Investigators in Canada cite shortcomings in baggage screening procedures and employee training. A second bomb, intended to blow up another Air India 747 on the same day, detonates prematurely in Tokyo before being loaded aboard.

6. *August 19, 1980.* A Saudia L-1011 bound for Karachi returns to Riyadh, Saudi Arabia, following an in-flight fire just after departure. For reasons never understood, the crew takes its time after a safe touchdown, rolling to the far end of the runway before stopping. No evacuation is commenced, and the airplane sits with engines running for more than three minutes. Before the inadequately equipped rescue workers can open any doors, all 301 people die as a flash fire consumes the cabin.

7. *July 3, 1988.* An Airbus A300 operated by Iran Air is shot down over the Straits of Hormuz by the U.S. Navy destroyer *Vincennes*.

The crew of the *Vincennes*, distracted by an ongoing gunbattle, mistakes the A300 for a hostile aircraft and destroys it with two missiles. None of the 290 occupants survive.

8. *May 25, 1979.* As an American Airlines DC-10 lifts from the runway at Chicago's O'Hare airport, an engine detaches and seriously damages a wing. Before the crew can make sense of what's happened, the airplane rolls 90 degrees and disintegrates in a fireball. With 273 fatalities, this remains the worst-ever crash on U.S. soil. Both the engine pylon design and airline maintenance procedures are faulted, and all DC-10s are temporarily grounded.

9. *December 21, 1988.* Two Libyan agents are later held responsible for planting a bomb on Pan American flight 103, which blows up in the evening sky over Lockerbie, Scotland, killing 270 people, including eleven on the ground.

10. *September 1, 1983.* Korean Air Lines flight KL007, a 747 carrying 269 passengers and crew from New York to Seoul (with a technical stop in Anchorage) is shot from the air by a Soviet fighter after drifting off course—and into Soviet airspace—near Sakhalin Island in the North Pacific. Investigators attribute the mysterious deviation to "a considerable degree of lack of alertness and attentiveness on the part of the flight crew."

These accidents comprise twelve airplanes and ten airlines. Pan Am played a role in two of them, as did the lesser-known Saudia (now called Saudi Arabian Airlines). In Saudia's case, the crew was absolved in the midair collision *(see number 3)*, but acted inexplicably in the fire at Riyadh *(see number 6)*. An interesting breakdown also includes:

Number of Boeing 747s involved in the ten crashes: 7

Number resulting from terrorist sabotage or that were shot down mistakenly: 4

Number that occurred in the United States: 1

Number that occurred prior to 1974: 0

Number that occurred during the 1970s or 1980s: 9

Number in which pilot error was cited as a direct or contributing cause: 3

Number that crashed as direct result of mechanical failure: 3

Interesting, but reducing these events to abstraction gets slithery. One could surmise the 747 is the most dangerous plane in the sky, neglecting that it carries the greatest number of passengers. Still we find some interesting and unexpected points, not the least of which is the lack of crew culpability in all but three of the disasters. Design flaws in the case of the DC-10 catastrophes in Chicago and Paris, for their part, play into fears of bizarre mechanical failures (usually diagnosed by this same author as irrational). Those of you solicitous for some corporate malfeasance can cite the mistakes of JAL, and all of us can sigh nervously when remembering the bombings against Pan Am and Air India.

What were your experiences on September 11, 2001, and how, from a pilot's take, has flying changed since then?

On the Tuesday morning when everything happened, I was dead-heading from Boston to a work assignment in Florida. My airplane took off only seconds after American's flight 11. I had watched it back away from gate 25 at Logan's terminal B and begin to taxi.

About halfway to Florida we started descending. Because of a "security issue," our captain told us, we, along with many other airplanes, would be diverting immediately. Pilots are polished pros when it comes to dishing out semicomforting euphemisms, and this little gem would be the most laughable understatement I've ever heard a comrade utter. Our new destination was Charleston, South Carolina. I figured a bomb threat had been called in. My worry was not of war and smoldering devastation; my worry was being late for work. It wasn't until I joined a crowd of passengers in Charleston, clustered around a TV in a concourse restaurant, that I learned what was going on.

I'm watching the video of the second airplane, shot from the ground, apparently with somebody's camcorder in a kind of twenty-first-century Zapruder film. The picture swings left, picks up the United 767 moving swiftly. The plane rocks, lifts its nose, and like a charging, pissed-off bull making a run at a fear-frozen matador, drives itself into the very center of the south tower. The airplane simply vanishes. For a fraction of a second there is no falling debris, no smoke, no fire, no movement. It's as though the plane has been swallowed by a skyscraper of liquid. Then, from within, you see the white-hot explosion and spewing expulsion of fire and matter.

Had the airplanes crashed, blown up, and reduced the upper halves of those buildings to burned-out hulks, the whole event would nonetheless have clung to the realm of believability. It was the groaning *implosion*, and the clouds of wreckage funneling like pyroclastic tornadoes through the canyons of lower Manhattan, that catapulted the event from ordinary disaster to pure historical infamy. They *fell down*. The sight of those ugly, magnificent towers collapsing onto themselves is the most sublimely terrifying thing I have ever seen.

In the twin ten-second bursts it took them to fall, I knew *something* about the business of flying planes was changed for good. And pilots, like firemen, policemen, and everyone else whose professions had been implicated, had no choice but to take things, well, personally. Four on-duty crews—eight flight officers in total—were victims. They were disrespected in the worst way, killed after their beloved machines were stolen from under them and driven into buildings. John Ogonowski comes to mind, the good-guy captain of American 11. Of the thousands of people victimized that day, Captain Ogonowski was figuratively, if not literally, the first of them. He lived in my home state. His funeral made the front page, where he was eulogized for philanthropic work with local Cambodian immigrants. I'd be annoyingly melodramatic to say I feel a bond or kinship with these eight men, but I did feel an underlying—and wrenching—empathy. I can understand, maybe, what it must have been like. I can *picture* things unfolding—from the storming of the cockpit to imagining Atta's hands on the thrust levers just before impact.

So people ask now, "What's different?" Maybe I'm more philosophical than many of my peers, but at heart the changes aren't of the quantifiable kind: security, cockpit doors, baggage screening, and the like. It's more sinister and intangible—something that can't be armored, upgraded, or fenced in by razor wire. It's a state of mind—a state of unease, disappointment, and anger. Anger to have had our industry taken advantage of so, our planes so brazenly stolen, coworkers fooled, killed, and thousands more thrown out of work. What drives it home, however, are the same pains and inconveniences now faced by passengers: long lines, angst, and unpleasantness in the terminals.

It'd be hyperbole of the worst order to speak of "lost innocence" or the world being changed forever. The destruction we saw on September 11, while certainly awful, could have been worse and was not on par with the trumpets of Judgment Day. But yes, for sure, flying is different now. As with the fallout from any trauma, we hope the more uncomfortable—and unnecessary—aspects of this difference are remedied in time. It will take a while, I suppose, for things to settle and reach whatever state of permanence they're destined for. In the meantime, pilots try hard to maintain standards of professionalism and safety in an environment running a gamut from justified apprehension to outright silliness. Like the rest of you, we were cast into a fray we wanted no part in.

We occasionally hear of the dangers of flying aboard certain foreign airlines. Are such fears justified?

By the mid-1990s fifty million Americans were flying foreign airlines to or from the United States each year. These range from the highly respected Lufthansa, British Airways, and Qantas, to names like Uzbekistan Airways and Biman Bangladesh. Many crews from Asia, South America, and Africa train at facilities in the United States and Western Europe, frequently under the contracted auspices of our best known airlines, using their simulators and instructors. But over the years, a spate of notable accidents has raised the specter of some unbelievably poor decision making on the part of foreign flight crews. One of the greatest hits of the pilot training video circuit, for example, is the morbidly hilarious reenactment of the Saudia L-1011 fire in 1980. And possibly most notorious was the apparent suicide crash of an EgyptAir 767 in 1999.

Two of the more dubious reputations belong to Taiwan's China Airlines and Seoul-based Korean Air. China Airlines (not to be confused with Air China of the mainland) has suffered twelve fatal accidents in the past thirty-four years, a rate well out of kilter with its overall size. Korean Air hasn't fared much better, and in 1999 had a code-sharing arrangement with Delta temporarily severed after the latest in a string of incidents (the code-share was reinstated by 2002 after implementation of tougher policies). Other sore thumbs are Indian Airlines (not to be mistaken with Air India), with fifteen deadly events since 1970, and Philippine Airlines, with eight.

But in a business where safety is measured by tiny differences in percentage points, *less* safe and *un*safe are entirely different things. Often enough, and happily so, comparing these kinds of statistics is an exercise in hairsplitting. Applying our own intense criteria to these companies might deem their records unacceptable; a fatal event every couple of years is comparatively awful. But when a given airline is responsible for hundreds—or thousands—of departures daily, you get a sense of the minutiae at hand. Raw crash data would misleadingly show American Airlines and United Airlines ranking with the worst, not accounting for their vast networks and frequencies.

One of the worst legacies belongs to Russia's Aeroflot. Put a check mark next to Aeroflot for each accident, and it looks pretty bad. But consider that Aeroflot was, at its peak, by far the largest carrier in the world, with a size approaching that of the largest free-world majors *combined*. And today, still maligned and thought to have a surplus of aging rustbuckets, Aeroflot (considerably smaller, having been splintered into myriad independents) has a younger roster than most.

Even most lesser-known foreign airlines are nothing to sweat. Many are surprisingly dependable and some have downright exemplary histories. A list of those fatality-free since 1970 includes several that, by name alone, are prone to cause an eyebrow arch: Tunis Air, Ghana Airways, Oman Air, Syrianair, and Air Jamaica. Allowing for one or two mishaps, the list expands immensely. To find anything close to a genuinely dangerous airline, one would have to break out the machete and scour the depths of equatorial Africa, or perhaps hitch a ride on a Somali cargo plane. "Americans have no reason to be afraid of foreign carriers," says Robert Booth of Aviation Management Services, a consulting firm in Miami. "Plenty of these companies have cultures of safety that meet or exceed our own," he points out.

Data shows the most dangerous places to fly are deep South and Central America and sub-Saharan Africa, where scores of small companies operate without anywhere near the oversight or resources of our own. But there's a tendency to dump the baby with the bathwater. There are critical differences between the modern fleets and professional training of, for instance, South African Airways and, say, a third-tier airline in northern Nigeria. Would I avoid a ride on South African, EgyptAir, or Royal Air Maroc? No, and I've flown on each of those.

Frankly, in certain regions I'd be more comfortable with a local carrier that knows its territory and the quirks of flying there. One example I love to cite is LAB—Lloyd Aero Boliviano—the national airline of the poorest country in South America. Founded in 1925, LAB plies the treacherous peaks of the Andes in and out of La Paz, the planet's highest commercial airport. Since 1969, LAB has suffered two fatal crashes on scheduled passenger runs, killing a total of thirty-six people. This is not a mainstay airline, but two crashes in thirty-four years amidst jagged mountains and the hazards of the high *Altiplano*, is outstanding. Does that mean a company like LAB is safer, or even as safe, statistically, as our largest American or European airlines? No, not necessarily. The greater deduction is that *both* are trustworthy.

The FAA, whose penchant for safety is outdone only by a

fondness for annoying acronyms, has come up with the International Aviation Safety Assessment (IASA) program to judge standards of other countries, using criteria based on ICAO (International Civil Aviation Organization) guidelines. ICAO (*eye-kay-oh*) is the civil aviation branch of the United Nations. Classifications are awarded to nations themselves and not to specific airlines. Category 1 status goes to those who meet the mark, and Category 2 to those who don't. Countries in Category 2 do not "provide safety oversight of air carrier operators in accordance with the minimum safety standards."

Because the categories pertain to countries and not individual airlines, and because the restrictions apply unilaterally, IASA has its critics. Category 2 airlines can still operate to and from the United States, but may not add capacity. Yet reciprocal service is unaffected. Hence, if Venezuela's Aeropostal is embargoed from adding round trips in the busy Miami-Caracas market, American, United, Delta, or Continental are happy to jump in.

Robert Booth finds the program's logic badly flawed. "If a country's oversight is supposedly inadequate, how come our airlines can fly there without penalty, but theirs can't fly here?" Booth and others recommend a bilateral capacity freeze to level the field and encourage governments to meet better standards.

But taking this a step further, don't you think there are cultural differences that might lend themselves to the safety of a country's airline?

Myths and misconceptions persist with regard to foreign airline safety. The psychology at work here can be complex, but in many ways it comes down to the tendency to invoke a certain conceit towards things from other shores. The term "foreign carrier" has come to be a collectively derogatory label.

Rumors that European crews are allowed to drink alcohol with their meals, for instance, circulate even among pilots. Another circulated anecdote is that of a foreign crew intentionally ignoring the cries of a jet's warning system because the computerized voice was that of a woman. Rather than be told what to do by some uppity safety device, they crashed. Apocryphal, probably, but I can vouch for a couple of less dramatic stories.

Beyond acts of god, there are only two things, alone or in combination, that can bring down an airplane: a failure of things mechanical or a failure of things human. A careful look at the numbers of the past few decades shows a more even split than you might imagine, but accident records nonetheless prove there's a lot more to running a safe operation than buying the newest or most expensive equipment. Safety runs deeper than the shine of new aluminum and deeper than technology outright.

The tangibles of technology and logistical resources are easily addressed, while the long history of accident investigation has filled the pilot's lexicon with catchphrases like "CRM" (Crew Resource Management), which are an ivory tower way of saying, "The pilot did it."

But *why* did the pilot do it? And here's where things get messy, because in the backs of our minds lurks a suspicion—one that suggests a pilot's cultural, or even religious, background might be a weak link in the safety chain. People of all nations tend to project cultural biases onto situations they don't understand and people they've never met. Although many Stateside crews have committed infamous blunders, we tend to judge our own pilots' actions through a quasi-scientific veil of human factors and CRM, while dismissing similar behavior by foreigners as blatantly irresponsible or stupid. But it can happen *anywhere*, to any airline.

The point is not to claim that all airlines are on equal footing, but marginalizing another country's airline by virtue of assumed cultural superiority is somewhere between shallow and shameful.

Acknowledging statistical differences is one thing; perpetuating nonsense is something else. Be very skeptical of information—even seemingly lucid firsthand reckonings—that you come across on the Internet. Levels of inaccuracy and distortion are extremely high, even at ordinarily reputable sites. I expect the more hardcore readers of Lonely Planet, to specify one case, are among the most experienced travelers in the world. Yet its "Thorn Tree" posting site—an online forum where supposedly savvy travelers exchange information—is rampant with misinformation.

Is it true that Qantas, the Australian airline, has never suffered a fatal accident?

Yes, although Qantas is a relatively small airline (138 tails in 2002), and historically a strong percentage of its flights have been the long-range, intercontinental variety. This equals fewer takeoffs and landings, which is when most accidents occur. What sets the Aussies apart, however, is that their national airline, Queensland

and Northern Territory Aerial Services (QANTAS) dates to 1920 and is one of the oldest.

All well and good, but branding their exemplary record as world's safest is wholly subjective. The list of airlines who've gone fatality free over at least the past thirty years, as we've seen, is surprisingly extensive. Presence of an accident or two, the causes of which might be anything from pilot error to terrorism, does not establish a pathology of incompetence, and should not imply an airline is any more dangerous than another.

I especially roll my eyes when the attendants go through the life vest drill. Has anyone ever survived a water landing by donning a vest or using a raft?

"Water landing" is a snarky contradiction, but over the decades a handful of airliners have found themselves, through one mishap or another, in lake, river, or sea. At least two of these—the 1970 ditching of a DC-9 in the Caribbean, and a 1963 Aeroflot splashdown near Leningrad, were controlled impacts with many survivors.

During the safety demo, passengers (those actually listening) are prone to envision a Hollywood-style ditching with icy seas, foam-topped swells, and maybe a merchant ship coming to the rescue. And if your flight is over land the whole way, well why bother? Keep in mind that planes have overshot, undershot, or otherwise parted company with runways and ended up in the harbor at a coastal airport, sometimes without leaving the ground. If you're flying from New York to Phoenix and you're smirking as the attendant blows into that plastic tube, remember that twice since the late 1980s jets went off the end of a runway at La Guardia and ended up in the bay.

I'd bet the house, if I had one, that it won't ever happen, but if you're in such an accident and have, as will be the case, not paid attention to the briefing, do not inflate your vest while still inside the plane, despite the temptation to do so. When an Ethiopian Airlines 767 ditched off the Comoros Islands after a skyjacking in 1996, several people who'd preinflated their vests were unable to move freely and escape the rising water. The devices are designed to provide buoyancy around the neck even if punctured, so if you're unconscious and haven't yet discharged the little cylinder, you'll still float with your head above the surface.

Almost every high-profile airplane crash is trailed by a conspiracy theory of one sort or another. Could you clear up lingering doubts and suspicions concerning a few of these?

It's hard to say which is the most notorious, since they stretch back to the death of Dag Hammarskjold and the heydays of the Bermuda Triangle. The modern era, if you will, of air crash conspiracies probably got going with the shoot-down of Korean Air Lines flight 007 in 1983 by a Soviet fighter. Since then, the Internet has become a sort of Dark Ages incubator of myth and misinformation, pseudo truth spread by the tap of a SEND button.

I've heard suggestions that the EgyptAir 990 crash was intended to be the "original" September 11, a suicide mission thwarted at the last minute by a noncomplicit crewmember. "The plane," one man explained to me, recounting some lunatic report he'd read somewhere, "had actually turned back toward New York." There's even a *reverse* conspiracy theory devoted to the notion that Pan Am 103 was destroyed over Scotland not by a terrorist's stash but from the effects of a burst cargo door.

The TWA 800 tragedy, at least in my time following the business, is probably the most mulled over disaster in the minds of the intellectually eccentric. Several years after the plane blew up like a giant roman candle in the July twilight off Long Island, the result of a short circuit setting off vapors in an unused fuel tank, the conspiracy crowd remains undaunted, exhibiting a marked, almost pathological refusal to believe mechanical trouble could have brought on the explosion. We've had a sideshow of at least four books and enough World Wide Web puissance to power a 747 through the sound barrier. Even mainstream commentators registered intense skepticism that flight 800 could've blown up the way it did. After all, fuel tanks don't simply explode.

Except, under certain and very unusual circumstances, they do. Indeed it's not likely, but it's neither impossible nor unprecedented. The airplane, an old 747-100 destined for Paris, had been baking on a hot tarmac up until departure, superheating the vapors in its empty center fuel cell (a 747 does not need a full complement to cross the Atlantic). Later, an electrical short deep in the jet's mid-fuselage bowels provided the ignition. At least two other fuel tank explosions have taken place. A Thai Airways 737 once burst into flames while parked at the gate in Bangkok, killing a flight attendant. (That's three cases out of tens of millions of departures;

please don't start gasping.) Per FAA behest, airlines will begin phasing in a system that uses nitrogen as an inert filler in vacant tanks.

Uncertainty took stage again after American flight 587 went down in New York City less than two months after September 11. The scenario goes like this: A bomb destroyed the plane, and the government, along with the airlines, fearing further paralysis of the economy and our collective psyche, decides to pass off the crash as an accident. No sooner had investigators begun talking about turbulence when the mongers yelled bunkum. I mean, come on—turbulence can't bring down a 150-ton airliner.

Except, in rare combinations of happenstance, it can.

If flight 587 wasn't a cover-up, then what happened? Reports of tail problems with the Airbus A300 have made news. Should passengers avoid this model?

On a Monday morning in November 2001, American 587, an A300 en route from Kennedy airport to Santo Domingo, crashed after takeoff when, to put it coarsely but accurately, the tail fell off.

Investigators first turned their scrutiny to the plane's rudder—the large moveable surface controlling side-to-side yawing along the vertical axis *(see moving parts, page 12)*. Black box analysis showed extreme rudder oscillations may have stressed the entire tail to the point of failure, possibly with help from a crack in the tail's composite architecture, which had formed years ago but was theretofore undetected.

These oscillations were pilot induced, presumably in reaction to the tug and tumble of a wake turbulence encounter *(see wakes, page 46)*. Flight 587 departed only moments after a Japan Airlines 747. The latter, bound for Tokyo with a full load of fuel, weighed about 800,000 pounds; it was heavy, slow, and climbing—the ultimate recipe for some nasty wake. The American A300, about half the size, was following behind and below, ideal placement to catch the brunt of the vortices as they sank. The jumbo loomed overhead, spinning a pair of invisible tornadoes like a huge, red-and-white spider. Smaller—much smaller—aircraft have crashed in the clutches of wake. But never a large jet. Could the wake have been powerful enough to destroy flight 587's tail?

What later came to light was a weakness in the A300's design. Namely, that overly assertive rudder deployment could lead to tail failure at a lower threshold than might be anticipated. It also came to light that Airbus Industrie had prior knowledge of the trouble. In a front-page story, *USA Today* exposed in-house memos complete with color rendering of a flailing A300. Had Airbus more thoroughly addressed the matter and warned operators, the crash might never have happened.

Regulators urged airlines to enhance their pilot training, recommending they include procedures to avoid rapid and extreme rudder deflections. "Rudder inputs by pilots can cause catastrophic failure," said NTSB Chairman Marion Blakey. "Full rudder inputs can jeopardize the safety of a vertical tail fin."

Pilots will chuckle at the idea of being dragged back to class to learn what is patently obvious, as a pilot pushing a rudder full-scale isn't much different from a driver on the highway suddenly yanking the steering wheel 90 degrees. What A300 pilots may *not* have known, however, is how sensitive their particular rudder's control units are to commands or how vulnerable the A300's tail might be to overstressing during unusual maneuvers. Now they know. Is the problem entirely solved? No. Is it safe to fly the A300, and are pilots armed with knowledge that should keep the jet out of future trouble? Yes.

When it all shakes out, the big American Airbus found its way, as most crashed planes have, to that one-in-a-million convergence of ifs. Two hundred and sixty-five people suddenly won the lottery that nobody wants to win.

What about other models? Are there any to be wary of?

We needn't launch into statistical somnambulance to illustrate the safety of flying in general, and not even the most brazen Vegas renegade would put so much as a nickel on the odds of a plane going down. If we delve into particular models, not much changes. Although this or that Airbus or Boeing is occasionally cited as having "one of the best safety records," virtually every airliner out there can make essentially the same boast.

In the aftermath of crashes there is often a rush to judgment. Not long after the 587 disaster, a group of pilots at American rallied for the grounding of the airline's entire fleet of A300s. Their petition read in part: "Are we completely comfortable putting our friends and family on an A300?"

That friends and family invocation is something employed

when making a point about safety. If a pilot balks at letting his grandmother or next-door neighbor onto an airplane, the inference goes, then he *must* have a point. While we shouldn't slight such a chivalric gesture from our polyester-clad professionals, it might be a more jarring statement if the *pilot*, not just his loved one, were missing from the guinea pig seat.

In May 1979, an American Airlines DC-10 crashed on takeoff at Chicago's O'Hare airport. A crack in the engine pylon, where the plane's giant turbofans are bolted to the wing, had caused separation of the engine during the departure roll. Detached, the powerplant bounced across the wing causing serious damage to flight controls and subsequent loss of the aircraft. *(See worst crashes, page 186.)* When, in the weeks that followed, additional cracks were discovered in more DC-10s, the FAA ordered the temporary grounding of the country's entire DC-10 fleet.

More recently, the crash of the Air France Concorde in 2000 was linked to the layout of the aircraft's fuel tanks. The plane struck debris on the runway, and an exploding tire caused a tank to rupture. European authorities—the British CAA and French DGAC—revoked Concorde's airworthiness certificate, and it remained grounded for fifteen months.

In both cases action was swift and peremptory. It has been more than twenty years, however, since the DC-10 fiasco, and the entire Concorde fleet involved barely a dozen aircraft carrying an extremely limited share of the world's passengers. Some will argue the system does not always react quickly enough or in the best interest of the traveling public. The FAA has long been accused of submission to the economic concerns of airlines until post-disaster fallout forces otherwise.

Cynics will refer to the saga of the Boeing 737, case study of an allegedly defective aircraft allowed to fly. There are almost four thousand 737s operating worldwide, and the aircraft—a twin-engine narrowbody—is the best-selling jetliner of all time. But the 737 was aloft for years with a known rudder problem believed to have caused at least two fatal accidents: the 1994 USAir crash near Pittsburgh and a United flight at Colorado Springs three years earlier. At least two nonfatal incidents occurred as well.

Beginning in 1996, the NTSB, which independently investigates accidents before forwarding recommendations to the FAA, requested at least twenty-two changes be made to the 737's rudder. Eventually the FAA ordered the complete redesign of the rudder's control units, and today all U.S.-registered 737s have been modified. The aircraft was never grounded. The enhancements were applied over time, progressively, while the FAA, Boeing, and the airlines worked together in solving the problem.

The FAA, which loves to posture as the altruistic guardian of the skies, will be loath to admit it, but in truth there is not, nor will there be, a true zero-tolerance policy when it comes to air safety. There is, uncomfortable as some might be with the idea, an allowable level of jeopardy, an acceptable threshold of disaster. In the story of the 737, a sensible, risk-evaluated approach seems to have worked. While the needed upgrades were hashed out, there were no additional accidents.

Call it a gamble. Threats are calculated and plotted, and disasters, while avoided at great cost, are anticipated and accepted. The annals of commercial aviation are full of mysterious, even inexplicable accidents, a fact, however frustrating, necessary to the evolution of technology and safety. Shit happens, which is a cavalier way of summoning up the inevitable when our fates are bestowed to the gods of probability and technology. We should learn to be more comfortable with this.

Is it true that the government had advance warning of the bombing of Pan Am 103 over Lockerbie but chose not to tell the public?

Having fielded hundreds of questions through my online column, and been regularly treated to delusional indignation from conspiracy buffs, I've learned to keep a lookout for queries that begin "Is it true . . . ?" My finger is reaching for the N key even before I finish reading. Every so often, though, somebody hits pay dirt.

In early December of 1988 the U.S. embassy in Helsinki, Finland, received an anonymous tip stating that a Pan American flight from Frankfurt to New York would be bombed in the coming weeks. Deciding not to publicize the threat, officials warned Pan Am and sent notice to embassies around Europe. All was quiet until December 21, the winter solstice and just a few days before Christmas.

That morning, on the Mediterranean island of Malta, just south of Sicily, two men smuggle a brown Samsonite suitcase onto an Air Malta jet bound from the capital, Valetta, to Frankfurt. The men are later alleged to be Abdel Baset Ali al-Megrahi and al-Amin Khalifa Fhimah. Megrahi works as station manager at Valetta's airport for Libyan Arab Airlines. His accomplice, Fhimah, was until recently that carrier's head of security. Prosecutors would argue the men are operatives acting on behalf of the JSO, the Libyan Intelligence Service. Inside the Samsonite and wrapped in a wool sweater is a Toshiba radio. Inside the radio, fitted with both a timer and a barometric trigger, is a Semtex-laden bomb.

Forged tags on the deadly suitcase inform luggage handlers in Frankfurt that it's to be "interlined" for onward journey. It makes the transfer from Air Malta to a Pan American 727 departing for London Heathrow, the first leg of flight PA103. At Heathrow the bag is shuttled to another Pan Am craft, a much larger Boeing 747. The 747 is scheduled for an early evening departure to Kennedy Airport, and the Samsonite is going with it.

Pan Am 103 is carrying 259 people when it disintegrates about a half hour out of London. The majority of the wreckage falls onto the town of Lockerbie, Scotland. Carried by the upper-level winds, pieces will be spread over an eighty-eight-mile trail. The largest section—a flaming heap of wing and fuselage—drops onto the Sherwood Crescent area of Lockerbie, destroying twenty houses and ploughing a crater 150 feet long and as deep as a three-story building.

Until September 11, this represented the worst-ever terrorist attack against a civilian U.S. target. Despite all the rhetoric that followed (Reagan was still president on the day it happened), no act of military retaliation was ever carried out by the American or British governments. Eventually, Megrahi and Fhimah were brought to trial in Holland. Megrahi was convicted and Fhimah acquitted. The

Libyan government, at long last fessing up to complicity, has offered cash reimbursements to victims' families.

With threats of terror so rampant nowadays, where does the Pan Am bombing fall into context? What did we learn and what have we done?

If you haven't noticed, airports are by and large intoxicated with security. To appreciate this with the nervous irony it deserves, it helps to step back in time. Lest we forget entirely, the '60s, '70s, and '80s were a sort of Golden Age of Air Crimes, comparatively rich with hostage-takings and bombings. The grandiosity of the 2001 attacks has gummed up our memories, and outrage wasn't really fashionable until the operatic fireballs and death counts of a collapsing World Trade Center.

Consider the Black September skyjackings of 1970, a drama of audacity not to be outdone for more than thirty years. In the space of three days, five jetliners were seized over Europe and the Middle East by a radical faction called the Popular Front for Liberation of Palestine (PFLP). Two of the planes were American—the property of Pan Am and TWA. Although all hostages were released, four of the five planes were blown up.

Between 1970 and 1989 no fewer than nineteen civilian planes were struck by bombs. A few of these, like the one aboard a TWA plane over Europe in 1986, killed a handful or fewer. Worst was the downing of an Air India 747 over the Atlantic in 1985, causing 329 deaths. In September 1989, hardly nine months on the heels of Lockerbie, came the bombing of UTA flight 772 over Niger. Destruction of the French DC-10, on a service between the Congo and Paris, killed 170 people from seventeen countries. (Libya has agreed to blood money settlements for its hand in the UTA incident as well. A French court convicted six in absentia, including Moammar Khadaffy's brother-in-law.)

By the end of the 1980s, European authorities were pressing towards a goal of system-wide explosives screening. In America it was a different story. For one, the airlines and their lobby, the Air Transport Association, resisted mandatory action. At the same time, the FAA was unable to settle technical issues with its chosen contractor over screening machines, nor would it dictate effectiveness standards for them. Various ideas were puttered with, but none were as popular as the cheaper, timeworn alternative: a two-pronged scheme of procrastination and finger crossing.

We were fortunate to interdict in the plans of Ramzi Yousef, who, in addition to his links to the 1993 World Trade Center prelude, masterminded something dubbed Project Bojinka, a plot to destroy more than a dozen airliners on a single day over the Pacific. In a test run in 1994, Yousef deposited a bomb beneath the seat of a Philippine Airlines 747. It exploded on the following flight, killing one passenger.

It wasn't until 2001 that a willingness to act was fully galvanized. In the immediate aftermath of September 11, conversations were always about sharp objects and guns; the cockpit door was the hottest topic in town, how to make it unopenable to anyone without a jackhammer. Behind the scenes, law enforcement and the FAA were assessing an altogether different risk. Along with many pilots, they were knowingly more nervous about what may be ticking beneath the floor than about hobby knives or scissors in a woman's purse. The time of reckoning had come, and the Aviation and Transportation Security Act, signed by President George W. Bush, at last decreed the examination of all luggage

Screening units have been deployed across the United States. Most of these are CTX devices, igloo-shaped apparatus that operate similar to CAT scanners. More than 2000 machines, at a cost of about a million dollars apiece, are needed to process more than one billion pieces of luggage spinning along our carousels each year. Deployment is imperative in small airports as well as crowded hubs. A device smuggled aboard in Bozeman or Abilene can connect anywhere and is no less deadly than one sneaked through at LAX or O'Hare. If the industry feels overwhelmed, it made a bad situation worse by resisting procedures, which could have been set in place gradually, for fourteen years.

How worried should we be about shoulder-launched missiles being fired at civilian aircraft? Should the airlines install measures to defend against them?

The hazard of portable rockets has become a hot topic, provoked by media stories about possible, even imminent, attacks using these weapons, which are small, easily concealed, and potentially very deadly. An estimated half a million such rockets exist worldwide, with more than thirty terrorist organizations and other rogue groups possessing them. Some have opined that all U.S. airliners—close to 7,000 total—should be installed with electronic antimissile devices, as are some military and VIP planes. A protective system marketed by Northrop Grumman would be available for about a million dollars per unit. It's doable, and the government has offered to pick up the tab, already pressing ahead with a $100 million feasibility study.

Nonetheless the idea has its naysayers, myself among them. What hasn't been reported, for one, are the weapons' technical shortcomings. As one ex-military airline pilot puts it: "These things are very unlikely to bring down a commercial jet. They are difficult to use and leave a visible trail, and when fired at short range are unlikely to achieve full performance in time to score anything other than a close miss. Seagulls flying off the end of the runway present a more likely and effective threat." Comments like these already have something to stand on. Two Soviet-made Strela-2M missiles were fired from a truck at an Arkia (an Israeli holiday charter outfit) Boeing 757 taking off from Mombasa, Kenya, in 2002. Both missed. Even a direct hit would not necessarily destroy a plane, as proven by a DHL Airbus A300 struck over Baghdad in 2003 and an Ariana Afghan DC-10 that survived a shot in 1984. Since 1990 two civilian airliners—a Georgian-registered Tupolev and a 727 in the Congo—were successfully downed.

Granted, we shouldn't disregard this or any other threat because it *probably* won't result in a disaster, and preemption is a welcome refreshment after our tombstone approach to explosives screening. The trouble is, we're again chasing the carrot of absolute security. Equipping every plane for every conceivable method of attack would be hugely expensive and then only partially effective, not to mention underscoring our hysteria. In this spirit, perhaps we should paint all jetliners in military camouflage.

In 2002 a British arms dealer was arrested in New Jersey for allegedly scheming to sell shoulder-fired missiles to federal agents posing as terrorists. The setting for this sting is what particularly surprised me. While an attack may or may not be just a matter of time, as a matter of *where*, I'm more confident. It remains my hunch that however portable and easy to hide a rocket might be, the target would be at a flight overseas. Since U.S. carriers no longer visit most airports in the Middle East or Africa, I look towards South America and the Caribbean as a logical staging ground. The enemy relies on porous borders and the ability to blend in, markedly easier tasks in South or Latin America than the United States, Europe, or the Pacific Rim. Where better to exploit the element of surprise than beyond-the-fray cities like Lima, São Paolo, San Salvador, or Montego Bay? In December 2003, a gang of Bangladeshi men were apprehended in Bolivia after scheming to commandeer a jet there for attack on American targets.

What would happen if the entire crew was incapacitated? Are there situations where this has happened and a nonpilot landed the plane?

"Is there a pilot on board?" As far as I know this has never occurred, except in a couple of Hollywood examples, including *Airport '75*. That means either it never will happen or is bound to happen soon, depending how sardonic a statistical analyst you are. A student pilot once landed a Cessna 402 operated by Cape Air, but this was a nine-passenger, single-pilot aircraft. Could that individual have landed a large airliner? Maybe, though she would have had little inkling how to handle even the simpler onboard subsystems. It's my feeling that no true nonpilot could safely guide an airliner, large or small, to earth.

Admittedly I'm making an old school presumption, and note how I say "true nonpilot." Those realistic desktop simulators make for some ambiguous credentials, and a fluent enough hobbyist would have more than a fighting chance *(see cockpit skills, page 139)*. Just ask Niklas Enggaard, who had no trouble flying and landing a full-scale Airbus A320 simulator at Scandinavian Airlines (SAS). Enggaard's training was entirely by Microsoft.

Since the attacks in 2001, it has been proposed that onboard software be developed to physically prevent airplanes from being guided into restricted airspace or over cities. Are these so-called "soft walls" possible or practical?

While we're at it, you might revisit the pilotless planes debate *(see pilotless planes, page 141)*. This is one of those things that keeps the writers at *Popular Science* busy. More power to them, but it's on par with the idea of establishing colonies on Mars: within our engineering abilities, extremely expensive, and then only vaguely useful.

In a way, it's an extension of something Airbus pioneered in the late 1980s when it developed the A320. That is, using electronics to help keep human beings from crashing the airplane. The high-tech Airbus does not allow pilots to maneuver beyond certain—and extreme—aerodynamic parameters. Apply some navigational extrapolation and you've got a plane that won't fly into the White House or the Eiffel Tower either.

Beyond conceivability, the real issue is usefulness, or lack thereof. Honestly, it's a lot of, to use a strangely apropos word, overkill—looking to outsmart terrorists by means of some needlessly complicated solution. A similarly overwrought idea is the one to make airplanes landable by remote control. Reading comments from people at work on these ideas, one is struck by how consumed and infatuated they are not with the promises of safety or practicality, but with technology alone. That's not a bad thing by itself, and probably a fine testament to anyone's devotion as a scientist or engineer, but for those of us riding in airplanes it's sci-fi show-and-tell.

An article in *New Scientist* magazine, for one, gushed over the soft walls concept with, "If [the system] sensed an attempt to jam GPS signals it would switch to other navigation aids . . . Soft walls would be immune to hacking." Hacking? Jamming? This article even talks about terrorists taking over air traffic control rooms. Sorry to curb the enthusiasm of any geniuses at Northrop-Grumman, but terrorism has always been, and likely will remain, a game of dirty, low-tech surprise.

In another way, too, it gets back to our greater national fetishizing of safety. By believing in a kind of manifest destiny of protection from every last direction of attack, we now wish to string coils of virtual barbed wire among the clouds. To me there's a beautiful and poetic futility to the idea of securing the very air above our heads.

A midair crash above Europe in 2002 spotlighted failings in air traffic control. How grave is the danger of planes colliding overhead?

On the first day of July 1986, when I was a twenty-year-old private pilot, I was almost killed in a midair collision over Nantucket Sound. My plane, a rented Piper with red and blue stripes, was nearly struck by another, over the ocean about halfway between Nantucket and the coast of Cape Cod.

I looked up, and there it was in front of me. It was a twin-engined propeller plane, a private plane not much bigger than mine. I could clearly make out the shape and colors of the human being in its pilot seat. My brain never had time to process any left, right, up, or down resolution to save us. Only luck—the slightest difference in our respective altitudes and alignment—prevented our two machines from hitting.

We were flying under Visual Flight Rules (VFR), using nothing more elaborate than what my instructor would have called "see and avoid" technique. Keeping clear of other airplanes, in the low-tech world of sunny-day private flying, is not a lot different, conceptually, from what's exercised on the highway. Airline flying is another story. In this realm, flights operate under "positive control." A flight is not only in the care of at least two pilots, but also under the watching eyes of air traffic control (ATC).

The queuing of airliners through opaque skies is routine, and with as much as five miles separating them, "crowded skies" is something other than the wingtip-to-wingtip swarm you might be imagining. Landing on parallel runways or crossing at high altitudes, airliners often pass within close proximity. But close proximity, in the meticulous doings of air traffic control, is measured in miles, or thousands of feet.

"We were landing at O'Hare," somebody might recall excitedly. "Another plane was right next to us. It was so close you could see the people inside!" To an anxious flyer, sensations and emotions revved, distances are distorted. Trust me, you have never been close enough to see faces through those oval windows.

The idea of airplanes coming dangerously close to each other, even hitting each other, is shocking—a virtual rape of the sanctity of the sky. How does it happen, and how often? In 1978, a PSA (Pacific Southwest Airlines) 727 collided with a small Cessna while preparing to land at San Diego. In 1986 an Aeromexico DC-9 plunged into the LA suburb of Cerritos after hitting a privately owned Piper that had strayed, sans permission, into LAX's restricted airspace. In 1996 a Saudia 747 was struck by a Kazakh cargo jet over northern India, killing more than 300.

For starters we should accept the inevitability of error. No flight is ever a perfect one, and minor, ultimately harmless errors occur with routine. It has always been this way, and shall remain so, just as the odds of your plane going down, no matter how bad a day a pilot or controller might be having, shall remain ridiculously in your favor. Corollary to these laws, airplanes do, on occasion, breach the confines of one another's space. Such incidents usually involve brief transgressions, a tangential grazing of restricted firmament. Sometimes a crew misreads an instruction; a pilot turns to the wrong heading. Almost always the mistake is caught. Safeguards are in place for just these trespasses—readbacks of headings and altitudes must be verified; controllers work in pairs; alarms are cocked and ready.

Almost every air crash seems to involve not one, but two or more unusual breakdowns. Investigators' final reports are full of uncanny coincidences. To ask, "Well, what are the chances of *that*," is to invite some unexpectedly retrospective amazement. In the case of the recent midair above Europe, the breakdowns included a missing second controller, a disabled alarm system, and even a malfunctioning phone line.

Independent from the air-to-ground link with air traffic control, airliners today also carry onboard anticollision technology. Linked into the cockpit transponder, TCAS—Traffic Collision Avoidance System, pronounced *"tea-cass"*—gives pilots a graphic, on-screen representation of surrounding aircraft (from whence comes its nickname, "fish finder"). If certain thresholds of distance and altitudes are crossed, TCAS will issue progressively ominous oral and visual commands. If two aircraft continue flying towards each other, their units work together, ultimately vocalizing a loudly imperative "CLIMB!" instruction to one and "DESCEND!" to the other.

· · ·

On July 1, 2002, over the Swiss-German border—the sixteen year anniversary of my own flirtation with mortality, right to the very day—a 757 freighter flying under contract for DHL Worldwide Express, and a Russian-built passenger jet operated by Bashkirian Airlines, smashed into each other at 35,000 feet. For undetermined reasons—the Bashkirian plane, a Tupolev TU-154 (a 727 look-alike), had been aimed head-on with the 757. Not an imminently calamitous situation just yet. The Swiss controller eventually noticed the conflict and issued a command, twice, for the Bashkirian crew to descend clear. DHL would stay as it was.

Meanwhile both airliners' TCAS devices correctly interpreted the hazard, issuing their own instructions in the final seconds. They told DHL to descend, and Bashkirian to *climb*. DHL did as instructed and began to lose altitude. The Bashkirian crew, however, disregarded the TCAS order and chose instead to descend, in compliance with the controllers' original, but no longer valid, request. Suddenly, both planes were descending and were *still* on a collision course.

Standard procedure is that a TCAS command, being the last word on an impending collision, overrides any previous instruction from air traffic control. Under the circumstances, following the TCAS alarms properly would have set the aircraft on safely divergent vectors. This protocol was not obeyed, and the two jets struck each other, killing seventy-one people.

To indict the Bashkirian pilots seems an easy call; TCAS commands always are given top priority and should not be overruled. Others have chimed in to remind us the planes should never have been allowed close enough to activate the warnings in the first place. Also true. No fewer than five breakdowns came into play: 1. the Swiss controller not realizing the collision hazard; 2. absence of the backup controller; 3. a disabled warning system; 4. malfunctioning phone lines that kept a German controller from notifying his Swiss counterpart; 5. the Bashkirian crew ignoring its TCAS command.

To whit, what are the chances of *that*?

Thus we see that air traffic control is not, and never will be, fully reliant either on "fail-safe" technology or the more subjectively reacting human being. A well-managed combination will be safest.

Is it just a matter of time before another collision occurs? Isn't our air traffic control equipment badly outdated? Maybe, but to recommend, or even demand, improvements is not to imply a situation rife with danger. The fallout from past accidents helped usher in the use of TCAS and numerous ATC enhancements. Instead of interpreting these doses of ill-fortune as harbingers of deadly incidents to come, we should see them as the price already paid for upgrades now in place. Our overall accident record is an excellent one, and stands as a testament to the safety of the ATC system, maligned as it is.

7

To Fly To Serve

· · ·

Mourning the Cheat Line

THE BEST AND WORST OF AIRLINE LIVERIES

I remember the day at Kennedy in 1997 when I first encountered the travesty of EgyptAir's newest livery. Gone were the earthy stripes and gold highlights. Up on the tail, Horus, the Egyptian sky god, was now floating in a tawdry field of blue. The colors of a nation's flag carrier, I exhorted my copilot, should evoke the imagery of that country. The old sandy tones reminded one of the Egyptian desert, with its great stone Sphinx and pyramids. The new EgyptAir seemed more reminiscent of the Vegas version of Luxor than of any true Egyptian imagery. Worse, the stark white fuselage brought to mind, well, not much at all.

In the past decade we've seen dozens of airlines reinvent themselves through fresh paint. Not since the 1960s has there been such an industry-wide makeover. Identities have been recast, usually at great expense, by big-name marketing firms around the world. The most prolific of these is Landor Associates, a company with offices in sixteen countries.

Ideally, a gallery of jetliner tails reads like an atlas of international symbols: the Lebanese cedar of Middle East Airlines, the shamrock of Aer Lingus, the rings of Olympic. The hard part, of course, is doing it attractively.

Today's is a more colorful apron, sure, but perhaps too rakish for its own good. There are fewer lasting impressions, fewer of the easily identified tails we once knew. It's bright, bold, and quirky, but at the same time cheaply temporal. Travelers today, watching from a terminal window, are asking the one question they should never ask: What airline is *that?* As stated by June Fraser, president of the Society of Industrial Artists and Designers: "National airlines change their identities at their own peril."

There have always been some notable rogues. Three decades ago, Braniff International was famous for dousing whole planes in glossy reds, oranges, and purples; pastel limes and powder blues. In 1973 Alexander Calder was commissioned to decorate the exterior of a Braniff DC-8, and later, for the Bicentennial, a 727.

As with Braniff's novelties, today's de rigueur relies on perception of the airplane as a whole, rather than a separate body and fin. Traditional paint jobs approached these surfaces separately, while contemporary ones strive to marry body and tail in a continuous canvas. The once familiar "cheat line," that thin band of paint stretching across the windows from nose to tail, is on the brink of extinction. There was a time when virtually every hull was decorated by this simple horizontal striping, now gone the way of those drive-up stairs and cheesecake desserts in coach.

If the overall color is white, the tail becomes the focal point—an axis around which the entire impression revolves. Clever examples, like those of Emirates, have powerful fin markings that carry the entire, otherwise colorless, aircraft. Similarly, Virgin Atlantic employs distinctive red engine cowls. Others go for a flying warehouse extreme—an empty white expanse with little or no detailing aside from a capriciously placed title. Most choose at least a partially rendered fuselage, avoiding the old-timey cheat line but escaping the anemic whiteness.

Whether stripes, solids, white, purple, or green, it ought to be done tastefully. That having been said, let's critique each of the ten largest airlines of the United States:

1. American Airlines

One of the few vintage holdouts, American hasn't changed since the early 1970s. Your author's first ever airplane ride, in 1974, was aboard an American Airlines 727, and I have a photo of myself climbing the forward airstairs of that plane. In the years that have elapsed, I have grown two feet taller, gained a hundred pounds, and lost half my hair, but an American Airlines jetliner looks precisely the way it did in '74, with its polished silver aluminum, gothic tail bird, and tricolor cheat. There's nothing particularly beautiful about it, but it works.

Archetypal, homely, unassuming. Overall grade: C-plus

2. Delta Air Lines

The executives in Atlanta have changed their minds twice now since the late 1990s, this time gunning for something flashier than the stodgy Delta standard. Textured bands of red, blue, and lighter blue (meant to suggest white?) unfurl across the tail like a giant shower curtain. It's also a near mimicry of the flags of Russia, the Netherlands, and Luxembourg. A fetching tail, but it lacks any meaningful symbolism—an eye-catcher for the sake of itself. The rest of the plane is an empty field of off-white, and Delta's well-known "widget" has morphed into a kind of frumpy, melting triangle.

Innovative, showy, geographically incorrect. Overall grade: B-minus

3. United Airlines

From spring 2004 United starts phasing out its dusky gray. In comes a cheerful new blueprint—and we do mean *blue*print—aimed to coincide with a summertime exit from bankruptcy. The carrier's emblem—the flowering, four-petaled U—is dashing as an abstract, truncated feather riding the tail. All it lacks is some garnish—a red highlight or two. The preponderance of blue gives the plane a vaguely unfinished look. And while bolder and more upbeat, gone is the understated grace of its precursor. There was something demonstrably civilized about the fully spelled "United Airlines" on the side of every plane, now snipped of its overtones to a lackadaisical "United."

Crisp, blue, blue. Overall grade: B

4. Southwest Airlines

For thirty years the uniform of Southwest was lengthwise fillets of red, mustard, and sienna. If it wasn't imaginative, at least the hues were desert-esque. Having expanded so far afield, the airline's look, if not its name, was thought something too parochial, and so it has been, um, refreshed. The roof of every plane is now a bright, syrupy blue, joining a neon red underside, the two delineated by an arcing, nose-to-tail ribbon of yellow. A Southwest jet looks like an overly rich dessert concocted by a starving child, or a vision of peyote-induced lunacy. Even the cowls and wheel hubs have been splashed with molten confection. In a bizarre nod to the original scheme, the tail's aft corner retains a swath of the old mustard.

Exuberant, profuse, may rot your teeth. Overall grade: D-plus

5. Northwest Airlines

The previous version, with its thickly layered red and gray, was always too rich, but the airline's circular corporate logo was a work of genius. It was an N; it was a W; it was a compass pointing toward the northwest. It was all of those, actually, and a smart and timeless design, perhaps the single best trademark ever created by our friends at Landor. Now it's in the waste can, bastardized into a meaningless abstraction: a lazy circle and small triangular arrow. It's no longer an N or a W, and it no longer points toward the northwest. It simply points. Which alone wouldn't be terrible, if only it weren't such a devolved incarnation of the mark it usurps. And it's not Northwest Airlines anymore, it's "nwa," in coyly affected lowercase. Only the sleek, brushed silver body keeps it from an F.

Tragic, ruinous, austere. Overall grade: D

6. US Airways

With its smoky, postapocalyptic gray and unadorned outline of the American flag, a US Airways jet is, at a quick glance, drably reminiscent of a military transport. But look again. The slight red accenting is remarkably effective, the typeface refined and elegant. This one's the winner.

Cool, clean, classy. Overall grade: A

7. Continental Airlines

Here's one that's pretty good with bare flanks (it's actually a two-tone white and gray with a slender stripe) and is immensely more pleasing than the overdone mishmash of red, orange, and gold that it replaced several years ago. Continental's logo—a sectioned globe against a navy background—looks like a PowerPoint presentation, and would almost be handsome if it weren't so immaculately inoffensive.

Crisp, light, ultracorporate. Overall grade: B

8. America West

Two things work against the Arizona-based carrier's funky identity. First, the AW emblem looks like an eviscerated plum teetering atop a mountain. And while the lightly sprayed fuselage jags allude to a Western vista—or a quivering sheen of heat rising from the Phoenix tarmac—the airline's typeface, in oversized letters down the side, can only be described as "Flintstones Modern."

Awkward, lively, cartoonish. Overall grade: D-plus

9. Alaska Airlines

Never mind that Alaska Airlines is actually based in Seattle. They get credit for sticking with their parka-wearing Inuit mascot, whose face graces every tail. It's a down-home—wherever home is, exactly—and effective touch. Revisionists have attempted to discredit the visage by claiming he's a rendering of Old Man Winter. Alaska's communications department assures me otherwise. Neither is he Johnny Cash, nor Che Guevara, nor anyone else people have suggested. He's an Inuit. But let's not get a controversy going or they're liable to change the face entirely. We could wind up with Kurt Cobain or Bill Gates up there. He's not the problem. The problem is the frightful fuselage writing, which runs billboard-style ahead of the wing. If you ever try composing the word "Alaska" on an Etch-a-Sketch, this is what you'll come up with. We assume the script is intended to look breezy or energetic, but it seems to have been penned by an Eskimo in the throes of electrocution.

Folksy, blurry, ethnically confused. Overall grade: C-minus

10. AirTran

AirTran is the former ValuJet, which made the ill-advised decision to retain its silly "critter" logo (a grinning caricature airplane) following the Everglades crash in 1996. Somehow a flailing cartoon plane with a freakish smile doesn't convey the best message after an FAA shutdown. Now reborn, they've tightened ship with an unorthodox banding of teal, red, and blue supported by an unusual beige undercoat. Basically it's the ValuJet outline, but with improved hues and a smart new tail. The undercoat, better off in white, is jaundiced and makes the plane look dirty.

Assertive, businesslike, refreshing. Overall grade: C

. . .

I wonder what Sister Wendy or Robert Hughes would say.

We'll do the rest of the world some other time. Until then people might assume the Europeans are outstyling us. But that's not necessarily true. Rome and Milan aren't exactly backwaters of art and fashion, but take a look at the clunky green of Alitalia, or the Spanish airline, Iberia. When it comes to liveries, it's tough to string a connection between geography and vogue.

British Airways earned a spot in marketing infamy when, in 1997 and to considerable fanfare, it unveiled its "World Images" look. A dozen or so unique patterns, each showcasing artwork from a different region of the world, were chosen for the tails of BA aircraft. Out went the quartered Union Jack and heraldic crest, and in came *Delft-blue Daybreak, Wunala Dreaming*, and *Primavera*. It was all very progressive, multicultural, and utterly hideous. Newell and Sorell, creators of the campaign, called it "a series of uplifting celebrations." A more cynical source called it "a wallpaper catalog." The queen herself reportedly held her nose when asked to comment. Eventually World Images was substituted by a fleetwide red, white, and blue that instead makes every BA aircraft look like a huge can of Pepsi.

My favorite belongs to Air India, with its sexy red swoosh and alternating English and Hindi script. Look carefully at an Air India jet and you'll notice how each cabin window is meticulously outlined with the little Taj Mahalian shape of a moghul arch.

We also could mention the "Sir Turtle" mascot of Cayman Airways, who looks like he just crawled out of a Bosch painting, or the tropical nightmare of Air Jamaica. But if I have to choose a worst of the worst, it would be the new Japan Airlines (JAL). Since 1965 JAL's trademark was a quintessentially Japanese one, a stylized depiction of the *tsuru*, the crane, symbol of long life and good luck, lifting its wings into a circular suggestion of a rising sun. It was graceful and unmistakable. The crane is being phased out and replaced by something so awful that it defies description, an insipid slash mark accompanied by a giant, bloodred glob—a Rising Splotch—oozing across the tail. I haven't been this disappointed since the U.S. Postal Service came up with that monsterized eagle.

Some of you might remember the old PSA smile. California-based Pacific Southwest Airlines used to apply smile decals to the noses of its jets. It was a DaVincian, ambivalent kind of smile that didn't get under your skin—as if each plane were expressing contentment simply at being a plane. (Alaska's Inuit is smiling too, you'll notice, but I don't trust him.) The PSA name, if not its good mood, has been retained by inheritor US Airways, and assigned to one of that airline's commuter affiliates. In Ohio. Deserves a frown if you ask me.

And yes, I have seen Southwest's orca 737, *Shamu*, and all the similar novelties. There has been no shortage of jetliners painted up to commemorate everything from ethnic identity to Bulgari watches to the Olympics. We could have done without Delta's Power Puff promo, or All Nippon's Pokemon, but the spirit is enjoyable in moderation. One of the nicest was an Aborigine-inspired Qantas 747 called *Nalanji Dreaming*, while among the worst were America West's indecipherable Arizona Diamondbacks promotion and TWA's *Wings of Pride*, a garish motivational tribute sponsored by employees.

By the mid 1990s this concept finally crossed an inevitable threshold, exploited to boorish perfection by short-lived Western Pacific Airlines, whose "logojets," decorated with ads in the style of a Manhattan bus, flew on behalf of casinos, hotels, and even network television. Calder represented the verve and style of Braniff in the 1970s; buxom cowgirls were the debased colors of air travel by 1997. Western Pacific is gone, but Dublin's Ryanair was quick to inherit the idea, and rest assured we haven't seen the last of the flying billboards.

Which are the largest airlines?

The following is culled from the 2002 *World Airline Report*, a yearly compendium by *Air Transport World* magazine. Despite my repeated plugging of *ATW*, they still won't give me a complimentary subscription, so the least they can do is provide fodder for an interesting chapter. Counts from regional subsidiaries—Connection, Express, Eagle, Airlink—are excluded unless noted:

The largest airlines in the world, ranked by number of passengers (2002)

1. American Airlines (94.1 million)

2. Delta Air Lines (89.9 million)

3. United Airlines (68.6 million)

4. Southwest Airlines (63.0 million)

5. Northwest Airlines (52.7 million)

6. US Airways (47.2 million)

7. Lufthansa Group (43.9 million, including CityLine subsidiary)

8. All Nippon (43.3 million)

9. Continental (41.0 million)

10. Air France (38.0 million)

The Big Three, as they're known, have remained in the same 1-2-3 sequence for quite a while. American and Delta were known to flip-flop until the former's acquisition of TWA, at which point it solidified an untouchable position. This is a first top-ten score for Air France, which nudged Euro-rival British Airways to eleventh place.

Earnings and losses can shift drastically over short periods, but the size rankings are apt to remain relatively consistent. Barring any liquidations or mergers the landscape will look very similar three, four, or even five years from now.

Another way of gauging a carrier's size is to use a figure called a revenue passenger kilometer, or RPK. One passenger traveling one kilometer equals one RPK, so it's a method accounting both for customer volume *and* distances flown. In other words, flying 100 people from Cape Town to London outscores flying 100 people from Dallas to Phoenix. Except, running Dallas-Phoenix twelve times a day can make up the difference. Frequency is the variable. Using RPKs the top ten get a little more international, with long-haulers like BA, Japan Airlines, and Qantas entering the picture, kicking out Southwest and US Airways. Delta falls to third.

You might be tempted to think of the biggest airline as the one with the most aircraft, but capacity differences make this reasoning specious. American Eagle has more planes than Alitalia or Qantas. For the record, American Airlines wins with 806 jetliners, followed by United and Delta with 557 and 547. Air France's 253 represents the largest non-U.S. fleet, followed closely by BA and Lufthansa. FedEx, incidentally, has 324 jet freighters, and UPS 228.

Which airlines are the most and least profitable?

The most successful airlines in the world, ranked by net profit (2002)

1. Lufthansa ($777 million)
2. Singapore Airlines ($601 million)
3. Cathay Pacific ($511 million)
4. Emirates ($287 million)
5. Ryanair ($259 million)
6. Southwest ($241 million)
7. Thai ($235 million)
8. Qantas ($223 million)
9. Iberia ($167 million)
10. British Airways ($134 million)

Plenty of stars on that list, but almost no Stars and Stripes. For those unfamiliar, Cathay Pacific is the airline of Hong Kong; Emirates is the pride and joy of the United Arab Emirates; Iberia belongs to Spain; and Ryanair is a low-fares maverick from Dublin. To pull some curiosities from the pile, airlines that posted in the black for 2002 include Aeroflot, Air France, Ethiopian Airlines, Pakistan International, Royal Jordanian, and Garuda Indonesia.

After September 11, the toxic ramifications of terrorism, war, and chronic economic infirmity went on to provide the industry's worst-ever financial scorching. Global losses have passed $30 billion, with half a million employees sacrificed. Swissair and Sabena, in business for seven decades, were liquidated. Colombia's Avianca, second-oldest airline in the world, declared bankruptcy. The multinational Air Afrique, dating to 1961, shut its doors. But through it all, the US majors have absorbed the full, staggering brunt. Of the ten biggest worldwide loss-makers for 2002, the top four—American, United, US Airways, and Delta, a kind of Four Airlines of the Apocalypse—accumulated $9.6 *billion* of red ink.

As the entrenched oldtimers gasp for survival, the rapacious low-fares opportunists expand meteorically. Between 2002 and 2003, Southwest, JetBlue, and AirTran banked more than $300 million in combined profit. The majors have been forced to brainstorm, and everything is on the table, from spinning off subsidiaries to reconsidering the viability of the hub-and-spoke concept that has dominated our air system for decades. "Business model" is the buzzword—how to rework it, discard it, start a new one from scratch.

Some are giving it a try with quirkily named low-fares offspring: Delta's Song, United's Ted, Air Canada's Jazz. While past alteregos yielded few good results—Shuttle by United, Continental Lite, and Delta Express all were failures—the difference, this time, will be an emphasis not wholly on cheap fares, but improved and efficient service. And if you think this boilerplate is strictly a North American craze, see Europe, where enterprises like easyJet and Ryanair have been capitalizing. Imitators are springing up in Malaysia, Australia, and elsewhere.

Another trend is that of outsourcing business to low-cost regional jet operators. When US Airways celebrated exit from Chapter 11 in 2003, it announced the "new" US Airways would be a smaller, trimmer company concentrating on short-hauls. This means greater dependence on RJs flown by US Airways Express affiliates.

A decade ago, turboprops were the workhorses of regional flying, feeding passengers—nineteen, thirty, or fifty at a time—from outlying cities to hubs. Today, sleek, high-tech RJs ply their trade in a wide swath of markets: Washington-Orlando, or how about Atlanta-Toronto. More than 2,000 RJs are in service on six continents. Seating anywhere from thirty to a hundred people, they provide an illusion of seamless service; a passenger sees no difference between American Airlines and American Eagle, United and United Express.

In fact these franchises, even those wholly owned, are run as independent units, with separate employee groups and pay scales. Wherein rests the appeal, as labor tabs can be laughably substandard. For now, union contracts restrict RJ utilization through "scope clauses," holding it below a percentage of a major's total business. There will be some hard lobbying to soften these arrangements.

When it's all said and done, the US airline as we know it may have ceased to exist. It shouldn't shock us to find, five or seven years from now, a domestic structure dominated by the low-fares mavericks and an enormous network of RJs. Already there's blood in the water. At any large airport, widebodies sit tethered to the gate like wounded creatures on life support. All around them maneuver nimble packs of Canadairs, Dorniers, and Embraers, either circling voraciously or going happily about their business, depending on how you see it.

People say the service standards of U.S. airlines pale in comparison to those overseas. How true is this?

For several years the corporate emblem of British Airways depicted a heraldic shield, beneath which unfurled the motto, "To Fly To Serve." That always seemed, to me, a noble enough ambition for an airline.

It wouldn't be fair to call service standards aboard major American carriers the laughingstock of the world, but it's something like that or well on its way. At a time when these airlines are sending out SOS calls and attempting to lure back travelers, it seems strikingly counterproductive to diminish standards rather than enhance them. Yet that has been the trend. At the same time come glowing reports from abroad, where by comparison life in the typical airliner cabin starts to feel like the dining room on the *Queen Mary*. Not only in predictably button-down regions like Europe, but in developing nations too. Take the example of a flight I endured in Peru:

LanPeru, subsidiary of LanChile, the well-regarded Chilean national carrier, is one of two competitors operating spiffy new Airbuses between Cuzco and Lima, the most popular tourist route in South America. On my first trip to the Andes ten years ago, flying here still had a frontier feel. There was even a company—Imperial Air—running Soviet Tupolevs. Today it's different, and instead of bracing for a fence-scraper in a banished Boeing or a Russian remnant, you can relax aboard a factory fresh A320. Thanks to this upgrade I'm unable to entertain you with tales of white knuckles, chickens in the overhead bin, or post-crash cannibalism. On the contrary, and emphasizing a reality that should be sobering to certain CEOs, my LanPeru flight was one of the most enjoyable in some time.

The boarding process was orderly and smooth. The interior was immaculate, and every seat had a moveable, Y-shaped headrest. Music played over the PA as we stowed bags and got comfortable (all right, it was muzak rather than Mozart—or Mould—but still). Newspapers were handed out, and I actually watched a flight attendant lean over a man's shoulder to switch on his reading light without being asked. I had to look around to make sure they weren't filming a commercial. A hot sandwich was served, and the drop-down screens played short segment features the whole way to Lima. This was not business class across the ocean. This was steerage on a sixty-five-minute hop in a third-world country. Total price: eighty-six dollars.

Palled by the grating tedium of domestic travel, Americans are sometimes astounded by the levels of polish and pampering aboard the best foreign airlines, where even the aesthetics of a plane's cabin are carefully considered. A few years ago, British Airways poured a billion dollars into revamping its interior schemes. "Colours are very emotional," says Neal Stone, a BA design manager speaking in Canada's *National Post*. "We want colours that soothe the passenger. Blues do that. Reds, on the other hand, tend to speed the metabolism." Somehow I cannot picture the powers at Southwest or United wondering how its carpeting might influence metabolism.

To be impartial, I gravely recall the knee-breaking seat pitch and treacherous cuisine of EgyptAir and Royal Air Maroc, but passenger surveys back me up. A selection from the 2003 Skytrax Passenger Service Awards reads as follows:

- *Friendliest cabin staff: SriLankan Airlines*
- *Most efficient cabin staff: Asiana Airlines (Korea)*
- *Best economy catering: Swiss International Airlines*
- *Best economy seats: Air New Zealand*
- *Best inflight entertainment: Singapore Airlines and Cathay Pacific (Hong Kong)*
- *Cleanest washrooms: China Airlines (Taiwan)*

In fairness, there's spotty positive feedback on intra-US flying. In particular, Midwest Airlines and Alaska, though small, are thought of fondly. Zagat Airline Survey consistently rates Midwest, known for four-abreast leather seats and freshly baked cookies, the best domestic airline. Aside from this we hear more or less neutral reports from first or business class, where it's harder for an airline to screw up. You can only be so uncomfortable in a premium cabin.

Current consumer complaint data holds Continental and Northwest as the worst performers, with Southwest and Alaska at the top. These rankings change all the time, but Southwest's perennial presence among the best shows us that complaints aren't necessarily an indicator of service standards. These days, not only do we acquiesce to intrusive security, we're becoming acclimated to lousy service. With expectations ratcheted down, getting home in one piece without your luggage diverted to Yellowknife is a satisfactory flight. Extravagances have been widely curtailed in the battening-down after September 11, inflight perks disappearing to offset losses and security costs. It's not an easy call in a business so bludgeoned, but this either/or philosophy is a prime mover of the differing standards between U.S. airlines and those overseas, where safety and service are not considered zero-sum variables.

Regardless of best or worst, many believe the airlines have grown collectively misguided when it comes to pleasing customers. How can they address this?

Satisfaction is less about luxury or faux-glamour trappings than about competence and basic comfort. Airlines should understand that most passengers no longer expect, or want, luxury in the old-fashioned sense, be it fancy entrees you can't pronounce or a choice of wines from five continents. Such things might be fun extravagances if you've dropped eight grand for first class, but they tend to come at the expense of more sensible, straightforward amenities for everyone else.

I'm known to wax on about the salad days of flying, but don't get me wrong: I neither believe, nor have I written, that luxurious pretensions deserve a place in modern-day aviation. People sitting in coach aren't covetous of a velvet-clothed cheese cart or a serving of grilled salmon with braised fennel and leeks. What they yearn for is a halfway comfortable seat, something to do, and for God's sake an occasional bottle of water.

Highfalutin affectations are at best artificial, and at worst downright embarrassing. In the premium cabins you've earned the right to some grandiloquent fun, if that's your thing, after handing over $5,000 for a ride. But what is a backpacking college kid in row 45 supposed to think when handed a cardstock menu promising "authentic Italian minestrone with garlic and herb croutons?" Sounds impressive, but he will not get a fancy meal. He will get a half-assed meal *pretending* to be a fancy one, served on a needlessly crowded tray overflowing with plastic wrap and cups. The kid is not interested in living out a bourgeois fantasy of the 1940s. All he wants is maybe some pasta or a sandwich. In much the way Burger King looks silly when it gives upmarket names to downmarket food, American and United aren't fooling anybody through puffy overflowering.

Interlopers like JetBlue are tapping smartly into our sense of dissatisfaction and desire for dignified travel. A ride on JetBlue is cool, clean, hassle-free, and the price is right. While not luxurious, neither is it without some flair. They are able to combine reasonable fares, stripped down amenities, *and* a dash of style, mutually exclusive as those concepts can seem.

People are quick to lump JetBlue together with Southwest, but there are crucial differences. Both offer good prices and convenience, but JetBlue's verve is intentionally more upscale. The jury is still out on whether their model is the stuff of long-term success, and it's important to note the airline was created with unprecedented financial backing—more than any previous new-entrant. This afforded a factory-fresh lineup of Airbuses and a high-performance infrastructure straight from the chute.

JetBlue's most popular amenity is live television at every seat. Not to be outdone, the 757s at Song offer organic food and forty-eight channels of digital entertainment. Song's mission statement: "To give style, service, and choice back to people who fly."

Already you've jabbed at Southwest a few times. If all you say is true, why does its less refined product consistently do so well? Can the low-fares concept succeed at both extremes?

I'm known to poke fun at Southwest, and if anybody is self-deprecating enough to absorb a waggish jab or two, it's LUV (to use the airline's stock ticker code, taken from its home base of Love Field in Dallas). This is an airline whose founder, Herb Kelleher, once arm-wrestled a rival to settle a trademark dispute.

Southwest is great at what it does, even as it pains me to imagine everybody doing it, and just as the larger airlines are stupid to ignore the sleekness of JetBlue, they're stupid to ignore the plebeian pull of Southwest. While we lament a lack of dignity in today's cabins, we shouldn't be nostalgic for the castelike constraints of the 1950s either. Today, for sixty-nine bucks, college kids and retirees can hop a Southwest jet from St. Louis to Tampa, Providence to Baltimore. Wasn't this, after all, the point of Carter's signature back in '78? It's without irony that Southwest deems itself "a symbol of freedom."

Let's all have a drink—something domestic, cheap, and served in aluminum—to the unpretentious, get-what-you-pay-for glory of Southwest Airlines. I'll make only one more observation, which is that Southwest should add a first class to its planes. That way they can have frequent flyer lounges too—where people sit around a room in the airport basement eating barbecued chicken on paper plates. (Kelleher would find that funny. I know he would.)

LUV them or hate them, Southwest is by no means the worst airline we've known. That dubious honor goes to the forgotten People Express, which also took on the self-imposed shame of being based at Newark. The no-frills concept has been around longer than we tend to acknowledge, and it does not guarantee success. Nothing better illustrates this than the rise and fall of People Express.

People Express grew from inception in 1981 to become the fifth largest airline in America and the fastest growing in history, having spun a network connecting both coasts and onward to Europe. By late 1986, with profits destroyed by mismanaged hyperexpansion, the airline was bankrupt. It was purchased on its deathbed by the infamous Frank Lorenzo and integrated into Continental.

Curiously, People did something only one or two budget airlines have done since, which is expand into the high stakes international market, offering scheduled 747 service from Newark on the East Coast and Oakland on the West, to London and Brussels. The New York City-London route is one of the most competitive in the world.

An audacious move, but even they weren't the first. The Brits had tried this in the late '70s, when Freddie Laker's namesake airline was making news. Sir Freddie, a high school dropout who showed the same kind of entrepreneurial flamboyance that would later make Richard Branson famous (and get him equally knighted) launched the Laker Airways "Skytrain" between London and New York in 1977. President Carter, prepping for his deregulation move, gave his blessing after Laker spent six years petitioning. People stood in line for hours to buy a $236 round trip, and Laker configured his DC-10s with a bone-crushing 345 seats.

Southwest, now in its fourth profitable decade, has always bristled at the idea of adapting its model beyond American borders, and probably smartly so. Cheap tickets, high frequencies, and all-economy services don't lend themselves to long-distance operations and foreign accents.

If Southwest Airlines represents, for better or worse, the Wal-Martification of flight, then Hooters Air represents . . . something else. Yes, I'm talking about the restaurant, which by early 2004 was flying a foursome of leased Boeings from a base in Myrtle Beach. If anything earns one of those only-in-America sighs of capitulation, it's Hooters Air. My first sighting was at Atlanta's Hartsfield International. Two girls behind me also witnessed the orange and white spectacle and hollered, "Oh gawd!"

This, on a considerably greater scale than Southwest, is an airline begging for some smarmy humor. The first Hooters Air joke I heard came from a man in New England: "In the unlikely event of a water landing, your flight attendant may be used as a flotation device." That's definitely funnier than my smartass lazy cracks about Southwest. It's also pointed out that Hooters would probably use the less politically correct "stewardess."

While I don't mean to spoil the joke, both cockpit and cabin are staffed by contract crews from something called Pace Air. This may or may not excuse pilots from wearing orange shorts, but I can't find any pictures. Not to worry, because two token "Hooters Girls," loaned from the chain's franchises, are strategically carried on every flight. What they do up there isn't totally clear, and I'm uncertain if this represents a promotion or demotion in the career of a Hooters Girl.

Before you sneer, the flight attendants at Singapore Airlines are still known as "Singapore Girls." And a few of you might recall the racy "Fly Me" campaign of the old National Airlines. "I'm Debbie," a prettily depicted National stewardess would say. "Fly me to Fort Lauderdale."

The Hooters slogan is a little less provocative. "Easy to Buy, Fun to Fly," it says. Something along the lines of "To Fly To Serve" adjusted for the budget set. Their aircraft are set up with blue leather seats and the company calls its extra legroom "Club Class," which is a brand once used by British Airways for business class. Hooters Air is about as far from British Airways as a Hooters restaurant is from a banquet at Buckingham Palace, but their planes are probably a lot more comfortable than most. And for some reason I see a copy of *Maxim* magazine in every seat pocket.

Hooters Air reports unprecedented numbers of passengers requesting aisle seats, and claims this is "for the scenery." Those at the windows have a view of mountains, while on the aisles it's . . . Well, only one of the views is real.

Which is the oldest airline?

Tracing airline genealogies is complicated. Many have changed names and identities or have blurred their pedigrees through ownership swaps and mergers. But most airline historians—there really are such people—agree that the world's oldest continuously operating airline is Amsterdam-based KLM. That's *Koninklijke Luchtvaart Maatschappij* for those of you speaking Dutch. KLM lists its founding date as 1919.

You will get an argument from a small company in Florida, Chalk's Ocean Airways, also born in 1919 and today flying a handful of small seaplanes. Let this stand as respectful acknowledgment of Chalk's longevity, but we're limiting the discussion to bigger carriers. Other pioneers include Colombia's Avianca, another one harking back to 1919; Qantas (1920); Mexicana (1921); and Bolivia's LAB (1925). Rugged terrain and lack of roads in some of these countries made them natural spots for aviation to take hold.

In the United States, Northwest is the oldest, beginning operations in 1926. Northwest's pilot uniforms toast their airline's origins as a postal service contractor with the words "U.S. Mail" in the center of their emblems. Northwest and KLM linked up several years ago in the first of the big strategic alliances, but for whatever reason never exploited what could have been an alluring pitch— their status as two of the earliest airlines.

Is it true no U.S. airline flies to Africa?

For now, no U.S. passenger carrier flies to any destination in Africa, nonstop or otherwise. The last to do so was Delta, with a short-lived JFK to Cairo, suspended in 2001. Instead we deliver passengers to Africa via our European alliance partners, while a handful of African carriers serve the States directly, mostly to JFK. These include Ghana Airways, South African Airways, and Royal Air Maroc. To the Middle and Near East, flights are nearly as scarce. Continental's Newark to Tel Aviv nonstop is presently the country's only representative service to the Middle East (you might make a case for Delta's JFK to Istanbul, but realistically that's Europe).

Several large airlines fly to all of the continents—British Airways, Lufthansa, South African, Malaysia Airlines, and Qantas among them—and their intercontinental business is booming. A few of the widest-ranging networks are an upshot of Euro-colonialism—Air France to West Africa, for instance, or BA to India and Australia—but if these airlines have anything in common, it's that none are headquartered in the United States. From New York, airlines fly nonstop to cities like Jeddah, Amman, Cairo, Kuwait, and Dubai. Others fly one-stops to Uzbekistan, Pakistan, Ethiopia, and Bangladesh. None of them are ours. Delta's New York-Paris-Bombay is about as adventurous as we get.

It wasn't always this way. Up until 1999 one could circumnavigate the globe on a United 747. Flight UA001 used to begin and end in Los Angeles, stopping in Hong Kong, Delhi, London, and Washington. Years earlier, Pan Am sold similar round-the-world connections, as well as tickets to Nairobi, Lagos, Monrovia, and Karachi. TWA could take you to Cairo and Riyadh. All of this is gone now, and we're content with proxy ambassadorship courtesy of our European and Asian partners.

Where we do choose to venture, we've cultivated favored regions.

Northwest and United are big to the Pacific Rim, for example, while Delta concentrates on Western Europe. American is by far the largest player in Latin America, while Continental runs a satellite base from Guam. This specialization is in no small way the fruit of previous mergers and hand-me-downs. Most of United's Pacific cities, and Delta's European ones, came from Pan Am. In Latin America, Pan Am, Eastern, and Braniff were the trailblazers. Braniff once ran a hub from Lima, Peru. As these entities failed, their networks were sold or passed on.

In the months after September 11 and before the 2003 Iraq invasion, international bookings on U.S. carriers were off as much as 40 percent. This was terrible news for an already sucker punched industry, as high-yield traffic (first- and business-class fares on long-haul routes) is extremely lucrative. Airlines reduced their international schedules, either decreasing frequencies or eliminating destinations entirely.

As of yet there has only been partial recovery. How long this downswing lingers remains to be seen and depends on the political climate and American mind-set. Frankly, the latter worries me almost as much as the former. Cutbacks in the name of economics are one thing, but at the same time they strike me as an echo of America's growing isolation from the world at large. I find it disturbing that our airlines no longer serve vast regions of the world—indeed whole continents.

Your dissertations on the airlines are very enlightening and allow you to show off your open-minded multicultural tendencies. All well and good. But what about countries that have no airlines?

There are plenty of countries lacking what we might call a serious airline, but it's extremely difficult to find any with no commercial operators whatsoever, even if it's just a copter or cargo plane, unless you get into the is-it-really-a-country game with places like the Vatican. As of right now there are no registered commercial operators in the Holy See, which of course has no airport.

Equatorial Guinea, to pick one, has seventeen airlines of one kind or another. Not to mention nineteen in the Democratic Republic of Congo, seven in Swaziland, two in Rwanda, and two in Niger. Guyana claims five, Cyprus and Belize four each. The Equatorial Guinea thing does seem a bit off scale, and brings to mind the way ships love to be registered in Liberia (one). Most of them are freighter outfits, and some have mailing addresses in Belgium, Russia, and the United Arab Emirates. Okay, but an old Russian rattletrap shuttling guns to Khartoum is one thing, you'll say, while a national airline is something else. True, but here too there is surprise. Even nations ravaged by war and unrest will make a point of keeping a namesake airline aloft.

Shortly after the ouster of the Taliban, I was pleased to spot an intact Ariana Afghan 727 at the airport in Delhi, India, evidently stashed there for safekeeping. Ariana's international services had been curtailed after UN sanctions in 1999, and eight of its planes were destroyed in the eventual U.S. bombing. Remarkably, within a year and a half Ariana took possession of replacements, including two ex-United 747s, and has resumed international flights to Russia, Turkey, India, and Germany. The airline of Afghanistan was established in 1955.

Iraqi Airways was founded ten years earlier, and in that manner of geopolitical kismet has primarily operated American-built Boeings. Their attractive green livery was once familiar to residents throughout the Near and Middle East, where the airline was among the most distinguished and reliable for many years. Following the 1991 Gulf War, sanctions forced Iraqi's grounding and several assets were hangared for protection in neighboring countries—Jordan, and even Iran (a bit like Saddam Hussein asking to store one of his personal jets at Andrews Air Force Base). The freshest resources list fourteen aircraft still to Iraqi Airways' name, though restart plans remain uncertain. Two surviving 747s are dubbed *Tigris* and *Euphrates*.

When battle breaks out, airliners often become a sort of civilian casualty. Iraq should know, as it destroyed several jets owned by Kuwait Airways during its short-lived occupation of that country at the beginning of the last decade. Defiantly, the airline had kept flying throughout the conflict. Kuwait's 747s were seen in New York even as coalition forces bombarded the retreating Iraqis.

In 2003, as the U.S.-led military campaign in Iraq unfolded, newspapers ran pictures of the bombed-out hulk of an Iraqi Airways jetliner, resting in a blackened crumple at Saddam International Airport. The tail remained intact, and I could see the wreckage was a

727. Noticeable was a missing—removed, not blown off—number two engine, leading me to believe the plane was derelict long before troops reached the capital. What's to be gained by demolishing an obviously unflyable civilian airliner is, I suppose, for the generals to decide, but I was saddened by the image of the dead plane, a gesture of conquest that seemed inordinately pointless. Iraq would need an airline again, and who's to say this old Boeing couldn't have been buttoned up and pressed into service?

Also traditionally loyal to U.S. suppliers was Iran Air, where more than twenty years after the shah, pre-Revolutionary Boeings continue flying. Somewhere in my photo collection is a shot of an Iran Air 747 taken at JFK in 1979, when I was a seventh-grader. The company is just one of several Iranian airlines.

Syria's only carrier, the state-run Syrianair, has more scattered loyalties, operating a mix of Boeings, Airbuses, and assorted Russians. Cringe if you want, but Syrianair has maintained a perfect safety record for over thirty years.

Rounding out the Axis of Evil comes Air Koryo, based at Pyongyang in North Korea. One of the last all-Soviet holdouts, Air Koryo features a graying collection of Antonovs, Ilyushins, and Tupolevs.

Something dubbed Palestinian Airlines was started up in Gaza in 1994 and since then has owned a handful of turboprops and even an ex–Turkish Airlines 727. News from Gaza is spotty these days, and the airline's Internet site flickers on and off. I'd venture to say their viability, if not their physical existence, qualifies as tentative.

Getting back to more peaceful regions, how about Air Namibia, with a 747-400 to its credit. Or Druk-Air, pride of the isolated Himalayan kingdom of Bhutan. On Nauru, a South Pacific speck with 100,000 people, you'll find Air Nauru, in possession of a single 737 and in business since 1970. Little Luxembourg is home to Cargolux, a globe-spanning freight carrier with twelve 747s.

The citizens-to-airplanes ratio also highlights cases like Singapore Airlines and Emirates. Here are two of the world's preeminent carriers, numbers two and four on a list of the most profitable, whose hometowns are city-states with small populations. Singapore's ninety-five aircraft constitute one of the largest agglomerations of widebodies on earth, a stupendous accomplishment in a country smaller than metro Philadelphia. Emirates, from a nation with half the people of Massachusetts, will be one of the first customers of the huge new A380—more than 40 ordered at close to $200 million apiece.

It comes down to strategic position, literally. By fortune of geography these states make excellent transit hubs along some of the busiest long-haul routes. They also happen to be quite wealthy, able to build the high-tech infrastructures and gleaming airports in which these esteemed brands can flaunt themselves.

Award-winning customer service doesn't hurt.

Similarly, KLM might be the oldest airline, but how does a country of fifteen million support a one hundred-strong fleet that includes no fewer than thirty-five 747s, especially with Heathrow and Charles de Gaulle barely an hour away. Answer: Construct one of the world's most convenient airports, Amsterdam's Schiphol, and encourage the world to connect there instead of the less user-friendly terminals in Paris or London. In 2002 KLM transported nineteen million passengers. As with Emirates, Singapore, and many others, that's considerably more than the entire population of its home country. Qantas accomplishes the same thing in relative isolation, as does Icelandair, where 1.5 million annual riders, a high percentage of them North Americans transferring at Reykjavik, outnumber Iceland's citizens by a factor of five.

· · ·

Every country would like to have its own esteemed airline. Not all can afford it, and many have gotten around the problem by joining collectives. Most renowned of these is Scandinavian Airlines System, or SAS, the joint carrier of Denmark, Sweden, and Norway. TACA, a popular airline from Central America, is another, acting on behalf of El Salvador, Guatemala, and a few other Latin nations. An arm of TACA has even spread to Peru, where the hitherto nationals collapsed entirely.

My favorite, though, was Air Afrique, ex of assorted West African states, including Senegal, Mali, and Cote d'Ivoire. Their green and white planes used to be regulars at Kennedy. Once a symbol of post-colonial African renaissance, Air Afrique recently announced a final final call after forty years. Another African staple since the '60s was Nigeria Airways, though its 2003 liquidation was less mournful. Notorious for corruption and inefficiency, the carrier appointed twelve chief executives in its final years, a few of whom spent time in Nigerian courtrooms.

This sets up a Bizarre Airlines of the World routine, which is maybe something we shouldn't do. None of us has any idea what an "AirTran" is, but that's nothing. We have, for instance, Russia's Kras Air, always just an H away from infamy. Or, even better, Taiwan's now defunct U-Land Airlines. U-buy, U-fly, U-land it yourself.

My flight one morning was nearly empty. The airlines complain they only make money when flights are full, so why don't they cancel the empty ones?

Airplanes don't simply ping-pong between the same two cities. A plane scheduled for Dallas will be needed there for onward connections. Or it may have an appointment for scheduled maintenance. Every flight is part of a vast puzzle. Hundreds of airplanes are at work simultaneously and airlines use elaborate algorithms to coordinate schedules.

An empty flight is never a good thing, but neither is occupancy always a good gauge of revenue. Even an underbooked departure can still be a profitable one. On international flights, premium fares in first and business class are the moneymakers, while those in coach can represent little more than filler. And down beneath the floor might be thousands of pounds of valuable mail and freight.

We left the gate on time, but a warning indicator on an engine thrust re-
verser required us to return before reaching the runway. Shouldn't this
have been caught in the preflight checklists? We conspiracy-minded in-
dividuals wondered if the problem wasn't known from the start and that
a decision was made to leave the gate on time, knowing we'd return, so
that on-time departure statistics wouldn't be affected.

While I'm not familiar with the thrust reverse systems of every aircraft, I can assuredly say that this type of malfunction, whatever it
was exactly, might not have been present prior to departure. Had it
been, you wouldn't have left the gate. While it's good to hear that
passengers have lively imaginations, they should probably be applied to more productive uses, because the sort of scheming you put
forth doesn't happen. You'll have to take my word for it. I realize
people start rolling their eyes every time a customer service agent
opens his or her mouth, but as I've written, the "lies" they tend to
tell are the inadvertent products of miscommunication or overly
simplified explanations, not active concealment.

In any case, the Department of Transportation is one step
ahead of you. On-time performance is determined by *arrival* time,
not departure. Airline personnel are often anxious to get flights
out for their own operational reasons, as somebody has to account
for a tardy pushback, but the official stats aren't gathered this way.

With all this talk of code-sharing between airlines, could you explain what, exactly, *is* a code-share?

Code-sharing is an arrangement whereby an airline sells seats, under its own name, on *another* carrier's flight. Waiting in a concourse in Boston one night, a woman walked up to me in a state of obvious fluster trying to find her gate. She was traveling to Europe, she told me, on KLM. I asked to see her ticket, which sure enough was emblazoned with the familiar blue crown of the Dutch airline. The problem here is that KLM doesn't fly to Boston and never has, despite large lighted signs and announcements on the airport bus to the contrary. "No," I explained. "You're actually flying on Northwest." Complicating things was the listing of two different flight numbers, one each for KLM and Northwest.

Welcome to the world of code-shares. All but a few of today's top carriers are in cahoots with at least one other airline, and many have joined in partnerships of several—supranational alliances like Skyteam, Star Alliance, and OneWorld. The idea is to cover as much real estate as possible, and the most powerful have at least one participant from each of the United States, Europe, and Asia.

And just as you can code-share to Europe and beyond, you can do so to Syracuse, Montgomery, and Eugene. This is important if you're squeamish about turboprops and RJs (not that you have reason to be), the vast majority of whose seats are sold this way. Call Northwest to book a trip from Memphis to Houston, and you might find yourself delivered to the door of a fifty-seat Canadair operated by its subsidiary, Pinnacle Airlines. Rules require full disclosure of exactly whose equipment you'll be riding on, so check the fine print.

The "code" refers to an airline's two-letter identifier assigned by IATA, the industry's worldwide trade and advocacy organization. Every airline has one. In the cases of our Big Three, for example, they are UA, AA, and DL. (These are technically part of every flight number, though in the U.S. we drop the letters. Flying Air France's Concorde from JFK to Paris, your trip was AF001.) In a code-share, a flight uses two (or more) of these prefix designators. To make it as mystifying as possible, the *number* part also might vary. Air France's flight AF718 is Delta's DL8718. Same plane, different letters and numbers (the 8 is dropped). If confused about who you're actually flying on, always look at the *lower* number. In the above example, Delta might have sold the ticket, but Air France will be serving the wine.

Why do our transcontinental "red-eyes" go eastbound and not the other way? And why do all flights from the U.S. to Europe depart in the evening and land in the morning?

Red-eyes leave western U.S. cities in the late evening and arrive on the East Coast at sunrise. In order to land on the *West* Coast at sunrise, however, a plane would need to take off from an eastern city at around three-thirty a.m. There would not be a large market for this service. It's a function of time zones.

There are scattered daylight flights from the U.S. to Europe, whereby you'll leave in the morning and get to London or Paris by about eight p.m., but the vast majority are overnighters. Morning landings in Europe allow passengers to connect onward later in the afternoon. Many people are merely transiting the first arrival city, bound for intra-European, African, or Middle Eastern destinations. After touching down, a plane will rest briefly, change crews and supplies, and then recross the Atlantic with an afternoon arrival in North America, granting plenty of time for connections there too. It sits for a while and then repeats the cycle.

This sort of system makes for very effective utilization of aircraft and is convenient for most passengers. It's replicated in other markets as well, such as between the U.S. and South America. For certain round-trips—Miami-Santiago-Miami, to choose one—flight durations allow early morning arrivals on *both* ends.

What are the longest scheduled nonstop flights?

In February 2004, Singapore Airlines commenced Los Angeles-Singapore service with an A340-500, taking the crown. Four months later the airline broke its own record by a thousand miles, opening a 9,000 nautical mile Newark-Singapore megahaul. Time aloft is about eighteen hours, actual duration determined by wind and weather.

Bring a favorite book (preferably this one), and leave your circadian rhythms at home. The effects of traversing ten time zones and the International Date Line make for some quirky logistics: Leaving LAX at 8 p.m., passengers land at Singapore's Changi Airport just after sunrise *two* mornings later. Leaving Changi at 4 p.m., they land at LAX at, yes, 4 p.m. on the very same day. Some advantageous winds and it's possible to arrive, as it were, before you depart. A New York-Singapore nonstop is in the cards for the fall of 2004 that will match or beat the existing pairing. The precise routing and flying time are not yet known.

Otherwise it depends if you're talking time or distance, and whether a flight operates nonstop in one or both directions. Trying to rank a top five or ten is bound to be met with bickering over a few minutes or miles. In 2001 United began flying New York-Hong Kong and advertised the 7,339 nautical mile trip as the planet's lengthiest. Shortly thereafter, Cathay Pacific announced matching service. Neither was profitable and both were curtailed, passing the baton to Continental, whose Newark-Hong Kong, of almost identical mileage, is flown with a 777 in about sixteen hours. While all this was happening, South African Airways claimed its Atlanta-Cape Town held the edge, while others insisted it was that same airline's longstanding JFK-Johannesburg—both going nonstop only in the eastbound direction *(see takeoffs, page 79)*.

I have experienced the JFK-Johannesburg route myself, as a passenger on South African's flight SA202, and can attest to the fourteen hours and forty-six minute ride having been less uncomfortable than you'd expect. I know it was exactly fourteen hours and forty-six minutes because there was a digital timer bolted to the bulkhead, triggered by retraction of the landing gear to provide a minute-by-minute update. Watching the hours tick by seemed a torturous proposition until a certain passenger was bold enough to tape a piece of paper over the clock.

Quaint seem the days, thirty or so years ago, when Pan Am executives sat in their Park Avenue skyscraper, scratching their heads over ways to make a 747 reach Tokyo without refueling. We've since closed not only the physical gaps between continents, but the ones between imagination and technology—perfecting not only the science of how to get there, but the art of doing so comfortably.

Traveling from New York to Chicago, I was surprised to find myself aboard a 747. Why would such a huge, long-range plane be deployed along such a short route?

One night at the airport in Luxor, Egypt, I boarded a four-engined Airbus A340, a widebody capable of staying aloft for more than sixteen hours. Where was I going? Cairo, about an hour away. Why would EgyptAir relegate its most long-legged plane to a nothing flight up the Nile? Why does Delta deploy long-range Boeing 777s between Orlando and Atlanta?

For any number of reasons, and this isn't a whole lot different from why a company might operate a big jet from a small airport *(see runways, page 89)*. It's about capacity and schedule more than outright capabilities of the machine. It may be a way to move a plane into position for after-hours work at a maintenance hub. Or, shorter trips may dovetail nicely with the "normal" assignments of the aircraft. A few spare hours between intercontinental services, plus their large capacities, allows these planes to pull valuable double-duty on a busy domestic segment.

And don't forget freight. Airlines derive money not only from seats, but also from the pallets and containers beneath them. One plane might be best suited for a route specifically because its belly space is most advantageous, even if ticket sales aren't filling the seats. A standard 747-400 has room for 6,000 cubic feet of goods in addition to 400 or more customers on the main deck.

Conversely, All Nippon and Japan Airlines fly certain 747s exclusively on their busiest short-hop domestic runs, though not because of cargo. Those are the choicest planes into which JAL can wedge an industry-leading, if that's the right word, 563 people.

How do flights get their flight numbers?

The assignment of flight numbers is more or less random, but airlines often give lower numbers to their more prestigious, long-distance routes. If there's a flight 001 in an airline's timetables, it's the stuff of London to Sydney or Paris to New York. Concorde flights were single digit affairs. Or, they might be grouped geographically. At United, transpacific flights are three-digit numbers beginning with 8.

Technically, a flight number is a combination of numbers and letters, prefaced with the carrier's two-letter IATA code. In the U.S. we tend to ignore the letter portion, but overseas it's used consistently. In Europe or Asia the airport arrival and departure screens might show, for instance, flights LH105 or TG007—Lufthansa and Thai respectively. When filling in your immigration forms before landing, you should use the full designator. Three-letter ICAO prefixes exist as well, but, as with that body's four-letter airport IDs, they're not seen by the public and are mainly restricted to air traffic control functions.

After a crash, one of the first things an airline does is change the involved flight number. There was no longer a flight 11 operated by American Airlines after September 11 (though, sadly, that Boston to Los Angeles morning departure had carried that number for decades).

Listening to air-ground communications over the entertainment system, I heard some airlines using code names to identify themselves. One I kept hearing was "Cactus." Is this standard or was somebody being cute?

While private aircraft use their registration numbers for radio identification, commercial flights communicate with a call sign, i.e. airline name and flight number. Clearing a plane for takeoff, the control tower would address, "Continental 424" or "Air France 012." In lieu of the conventional call sign, various airlines have adopted more idiosyncratic monikers. America West's "Cactus" is a prime specimen. Aer Lingus uses the classic "Shamrock," while at China Airlines it's "Dynasty." Others aren't so self-explanatory. People presume British Airways' "Speedbird" is a reference to Concorde, but actually it's the nickname of an old corporate logo—a delta-winged colophon dating back to BA's predecessors. A "Springbok" is an antelope, and also the handle of South African Airways.

Pan Am's "Clipper" was arguably the most famous example. Brought back to life by the recast Pan Am now operating out of New Hampshire, its use is not, you might say, politically recognized by some, and rings with a certain tone of non-legitimacy. Others from the past are New York Air's "Apple," Air Florida's "Palm," and

ValuJet's unfortunate election of "Critter." Winning plaque in the call sign hall of shame, however, goes to my own former employer, Northeast Express Regional Airlines, who in a fit of terrible judgment chose the first letters of its names to create the hideous acronym "NERA," pronounced, I think, "near-ah." Utterance of this awful word brought grimaces to the faces of pilots and controllers alike, and was changed after a few weeks, possibly by order of the FAA.

You're telling us that Pan American went out of business in 1991. But just the other day I saw a Pan Am jet here in Orlando.

The ghost ship you saw was one of several 727s owned by the Guilford Transportation Company, which runs an airline based in Portsmouth, New Hampshire. The airline? Pan Am. The name and trademark were purchased from the estate of the very defunct Pan American World Airways. Beyond the various blue and white superficials, and blasphemous use of the "Clipper" call sign, there's no connection between this outfit and the original.

Sound strange? This is a *second* resurrection. Let's call it Pan Am Three. Pan Am Two operated briefly in the mid 1990s, pulling the same trick and flying A300s from JFK before joining its predecessor on that big tarmac in the sky. There have been other in-name-only precedents as well, most of them short-lived: Braniff Three followed Braniff Two, and there was a Midway Two too. Today there are no Braniffs and no Midways, but there is, for the time being, a Pan Am. There's also a Frontier Airlines, based in Denver, borrowing the name of the original Frontier that flew from 1950 until 1986.

When USAir—as US Airways was called at the time—absorbed Piedmont and Pacific Southwest in the 1980s, these brands had been so admired that a decision was made to keep the names alive. They were assigned to two USAir Express affiliates. Suddenly, Pacific Southwest Airlines, recast only as the meaningless letters "PSA," found itself based in Ohio, while at airports along the eastern seaboard passengers could once again step aboard a "Piedmont" turboprop. USAir itself, originally called Allegheny Airlines, assigned the Allegheny name to yet a third Express division.

What are those numbers and letters for on the back of every plane's fuselage?

That's the ship's registration, which like a car's license plate is displayed on the exterior. All U.S. registrations are prefixed with the letter N, followed by a sequence of numbers and, more often than not, letters. A United 747 registration: N184UA. Note the UA denotes United Airlines, but this rule isn't universal. Other countries do it differently, some using only letters, others a mix. An Air France A340: F-GLZP. A Japan Airlines 747: JA8094. Often the prefix coding, which corresponds to each nation's ITU radio designation (don't ask), is intuitive. In addition to France and Japan you've got G- for Great Britain, I- for Italy, and D- for Germany. Others are random and inexplicable.

Registrations don't always change when a plane is sold, and occasionally a jet's letters or numbers can give insight into its history. If you see a 727 freighter with a registration ending "AA," chances are it once flew passengers for American Airlines.

If your beloved proposes to you in seat 5E, or you have some life-altering epiphany in row 32, and would like a frameable immortalization of the setting, jot down your plane's registration and pay a visit to www.airliners.net. This amazingly comprehensive database of airliner photography allows you to pull up not only representative models, but individual aircraft. Enter N334AA or N612UA and you'll be shown better-day shots of the two 767s that hit the World Trade Center.

I flew aboard an airplane that had a name painted near its nose. Are planes sometimes named individually, like ships or boats?

All airliners wear registrations, marked in numbers or letters on the rear fuselage, but some, in the finest *Enola Gay* tradition, also wear names. A few years back, United began calling some of its jets after various employees and even frequent flyers (imagine *not* getting an upgrade on the very plane with your name on its nose). If a plane has been christened in honor of something, somewhere, or somebody, look for titles on the forward fuselage, usually just below the cockpit.

Turkish Airlines names its spotless Boeings and Airbuses after Anatolian cities. You can ride aboard the *Konya*, the *Ankara*, or the *Isparta*. Flying Virgin Atlantic, which styles itself a bit more whimsically, you might have a seat on the *Maiden Toulouse*, or maybe the *Tubular Belle*. Austrian charter carrier Lauda Air remembers artists and musicians with, among many, the *Gustave Klimt*, the *Bob Marley*, and a 767 named *Freddie Mercury*. Air Namibia's sole 747-400 is the *Welwitschia*, homage to a strange desert succulent that grows in the Namibian wilds and can live for centuries. (I only know this because I spent two weeks there and saw one.)

You can ride the *St. Patrick* to Dublin on Aer Lingus—no surprise there—or try your luck on a Syrianair 747 called *Arab Solidarity*. (We assume the Iranian government's 727 *Palestine* will not be touching down at Tel Aviv any time soon.) South African Airways, like Turkish, concentrates on cities. To Johannesburg I rode the *Durban*, then the *Bloemfonetein* on my return. If unsure, I only needed to check the wooden plaque near the upper deck stairs, emblazoned with a crest and scroll. If done right, it's an elegant, ocean liner sort of touch.

Pan Am was the most renowned when it came to titles, all aircraft sporting a *Clipper* designation, a carryover from the airline's grandiose earlier years, when its flying boats pioneered routes across the oceans. There were nautical references (*Sea Serpent*, *Mermaid*, *Gem of the Ocean*), including a particular fascination with waves (*Crest of the Wave*, *Dashing Wave*, *Wild Wave*). There were nods to Greek and Roman mythology (*Jupiter*, *Mercury*, *Argonaut*), and the inevitable heaping of faux-inspirational piffle (*Empress of the Skies*, *Glory of the Skies*, *Freedom*). Most enjoyable, though, are the mystifyingly esoteric ones. Looking back at some of the choices, one wonders if Juan Trippe and his boys weren't tippling too much scotch in the boardrooms of their Park Avenue skyscraper: *Water Witch? Neptune's Car? Nonpareil? Young*

Brander? (Turns out most of these came from old sailing vessels.) And you've got to give an airline credit for daring to paint *Clipper Wild Duck* on the side of an L-1011.

When Pan Am 103 was blown up over Scotland in 1988, the only part to remain somewhat intact was the forward fuselage, from the nose to, roughly, the first set of cabin doors. It was crushed when it landed, on its side, but still looked like a piece of an airplane, which is more than you can say for the rest of it. This piece, as it happened, would become something of a news icon in the weeks ahead. It was photogenic, in a disaster-story kind of way—on the front of every newspaper and the covers of *Time* and *Newsweek*. There's detritus and debris everywhere, wires and scraps of metal, all surrounding this impossibly still-dignified chunk of a Boeing 747, dead as a door-nail. There's the blue stripe, the paint barely scratched. And there, just above the oval cabin windows in frilly blue lettering, you can still read clearly the words: *Clipper Maid of the Seas.*